"… *Going Off*, is a guide for African American Women on how to effectively deal with anger… The sisters offer a great example of two women who got mad, and then got ahead by doing something that improved the lives of everyone in their community… they reaped many benefits themselves. I've seen it happen many, many times. While some may think they have to fight their way to success, perhaps hurting others along the way, I've seen so many people lead happy and fulfilling lives of real achievement by focusing instead on helping others. It has happened to me too."

-Stedman Graham, Author, *BUILD YOUR OWN LIFE BRAND!*

What Makes Women Go Off

Adrenaline gives us the fuel to "go off"; however, after such explosions women may face hurtful consequences. We need to examine our style of communicating when we are angry and recognize when we are exhibiting unhealthy anger styles. Our anger can develop into stress-related symptoms from insomnia to cardiovascular disorders.

ANGer StyLe	ANGer ReSpoNSe
AUTHORITARIAN **When angry, the authoritarian sister usually has difficulty seeing other's points of view or feelings**. This person can be blunt and not realize that she is offending others by her words.	**What this sister must think about before Responding is:** "Am I thinking from a one-way perspective? Am I jumping to conclusions? Do I want to destroy this relationship by saying hurtful things? Do I need to cool down before I respond?

HIGH PROFILE

The high-profile sister is concerned with her image and may put on a strong front when angry. Trying to make the best of a bad situation, she will attempt to remain optimistic and sociable, but her body language often reveals that she's upset. The high-profile person especially becomes angry when she is not recognized or feels rejected. She needs to be aware of losing touch with her emotions.

The high-profile sister needs to think about the following before she responds to triggers: "Do I feel rejected? Am I upset because I'm not the center of attention? Am I feeling like someone has one up on me? Am I upset over someone else's success?"

PRAGMATIC	When anger is triggered, the pragmatic sister needs to check her internal dialogue.
The pragmatic sister is a stable team player Who is at risk of internalizing anger for fear of what others may think about her. Although this sister enjoys serenity, she is also at risk of blindly going off after holding in angry feelings for long periods of time. When this happens, she often has regrets about the incident because she views herself as the glue that holds her relationships together.	"Am I giving more weight to others' opinions than I should? Am I allowing my negative emotions to draw conclusions regarding this situation? Am I avoiding confrontation?"

INTELLECTUAL	When anger is triggered, the intellectual sister needs to consider the following: "Am I reacting to criticism? Am I blaming others or myself? Am I exaggerating others' shortcomings?
The intellectual sister likes to be in control and feels angry when she is criticized. She wants everyone to adhere to set rules and has a difficult time understanding why they are broken. The intellectual person is sensitive to anyone criticizing her, but at the same time she is highly critical of herself and others. This person must become aware of negative self-talk and self-doubt that could turn into compulsive thoughts. She also needs to become aware of alienating the people she criticizes.	

GOING OFF

FAYE CHILDS
and NOREEN PALMER,

M.A., M.S.W.

GOING

OFF

A Guide for Black Women Who've

Just About Had Enough

ISBN: 1-4699-1292-9
ISBN-13:   9781469912929

In loving memory

of our parents,

Alfred and Lur Lena J. White

CONTENTS

When I think about sisterhood, I ask, Am I my sister's keeper? I say, No, I am my sister. When I cry my sister cries and when I hurt my sister hurts. When I think about sisterhood, it is about being our highest self, it is being our most loving self, it is being our most peaceful self. So that when we move into the company of our sisters, that is what we bring. European consciousness has a lot to do with the breakdown of our sisterhood. With this foreign culture, male domination has taught us to hate ourselves.

We are indoctrinated not to trust ourselves and we are more addicted to drama, crisis, and chaos than we are to peace, joy, harmony, and balance. As a result, when you hate yourself, you cannot love your sister. When you are not at peace, you do not bring peace into your sister's experience. When you are not clear about who you are and what your purpose is in life, it is very difficult to see someone for the purpose that they bring to your life. So if we want to strengthen sisterhood, we have to become the most loving, conscious, purposeful, clear, and harmonious beings that we can be. As we become more empowered and centered, and clear the darkness, our sisters will be revealed and healed. When you move into a space with love and with peace, it is healing. For sisters out there in the world I say to them: Affirm yourselves! I am the Blessing, I am the Blessing. People are healed in my presence, for I am not my sister's keeper, but I am my sister.

—IYANLA VANZANT

Part One

GOING OFF

1 WHAT IS GOING OFF?

"Did you ever wonder why so many sisters look so
angry? Why we walk like we've got bricks in our
bags and will curse you at the drop of a hat? It's
because stress is hemmed into our dresses, pressed
into our hair, mixed in our perfume and painted
on our fingers."

—OPAL PALMER ADISA, *BODY AND SOUL*

THIS BOOK IS ABOUT how we respond when we're
angry and how we can deal with our anger to bring more peace
into our lives. The Million Woman March in Philadelphia revealed
how the spirit of sisterhood can be strengthened in our own communities and in our personal relationships. We can use our anger
as African-American women by going against stereotypical expectations for sisters to "go off" when stressed; instead we can
recognize and acknowledge anger as a catalyst for change in our
lives.

When Rosa Parks had enough, she had enough. Parks refused
to get up and give her seat to a white man because she was tired
and had just about had it. When we begin to make a positive
change in our lives, it doesn't mean that the results will come
instantly. Nothing is won without a struggle. Parks's decision
changed the course of history for all African Americans; when she

faced adversity she responded in a peaceful manner and held steadfast to her beliefs.

BLACK WOMEN AND ANGER

We became fascinated with the subject of black women and anger after Faye was interviewed about it by both a newspaper and a magazine. After receiving a tremendous response from the articles, we started conducting research on black women and anger, and we found that a book dedicated to the subject did not exist. There were pieces in several books that briefly mentioned it but that was all. This is not a complete surprise considering that the overall subject of women and anger did not become widely discussed until the late 1970s. If women in general fear anger in this society, then it is doubly so for African-American women. Why is black women's anger so different from other women? No women in America have a history of slavery except for African-American women—and the legacy of slavery continues to affect us in present times. It affects us in terms of our economic status and our social status. We learned early in the bullwhip days of slavery to contain our anger or face severe punishment, even death. On some plantations, conditions were so cruel that the death of a slave family member wasn't mourned because they knew that heaven had to be a better place.

DURING THE WOMEN and anger survey, we asked four hundred sisters: "Do you go off?" Seventy-three percent of survey participants said they definitely did and defined what it meant, not only in writing but also in their conversation. "Going off" is peculiar to black women when they become angry. From our survey we identified two different levels of going off: the sista sass level and the sapphire level. The sista sass level is the type of angry response that includes slanted eyes, angled body posture, tilted heads, and sashaying on about our business when finished speaking our minds. Going off sista sass style means brutally telling someone what you think—verbalizing what's on your mind. The sapphire level of going off is an escalated angry response that takes an argument to the extreme, which includes losing the perspective of the situation, becoming verbally or physically abusive, throwing things, and venturing into tactics that are below the belt.

In workshops we conducted on women and anger, we asked the question, "What is going off?" The first response was usually laughter, because sisters think of one of their going-off episodes and, as they reflect on the drama, they realize that sometimes they let themselves go too far. The sisters who didn't laugh generally exhibited an anger style that was harmful because they masked their emotions instead of expressing them.

Often sisters will let anger build up until they can't contain it anymore, and then they release the anger in an aggressive way. There are better ways to manage our anger, and if we stop allowing people to walk all over us without saying anything, we will be less inclined to completely lose control because we have reasonably expressed our views.

In our women and anger workshops, we also asked sisters to examine their perceptions of anger. "It's a feeling in my gut when I can't accept something," said one participant. "As the feeling grows, it upsets me more and more until I can't control myself. I have to lash out." Another respondent shared, "I feel the rage in my head and chest; then I clench my fist—I hate that feeling."

These sisters' descriptions fit our definition of extreme anger—an emotional and physical response to stress and anxiety.

In one exercise, sisters described their anger as follows:

- tension
- screaming, yelling
- frustration
- throwing things
- verbal abuse
- hitting
- controlling people
- internalizing feelings

Do you agree with some of the descriptions above? All of the above? What would you add to the list? If you agree with some of the words on the list, you may see anger as negative or hurtful.

THE STRUGGLE AGAINST STEREOTYPES

Proving our femininity has long been an issue for black women. Our initial entry into American society forced us into backbreaking daily labor, while we simultaneously struggled to love and raise our children.

Sojourner Truth had to defend her womanhood when she was accused of being a man because she had been forced to do a man's work. After slavery, African-American women felt unresolved anger. Sisters were searching for their spouses and children who had been sold and separated from them. It was extremely challenging to locate a child that was separated or sold at birth. Forty acres and a mule was a broken promise; when we were freed, we only had what John Hope Franklin describes as one kind of freedom. We were still economically enslaved. Split, blended, and broken families became a way of life for us in our beginnings as a free people.

Persistent perceptions of black women—from being loud and overly aggressive to sassy and overtly sexual—relate to the media's depiction of black women on television and in movies. The stereotypical Aunt Jemima type is the caring, nurturing figure whose purpose is to serve all others' needs. African-American women traditionally have been portrayed negatively in mass media with messages that tell us that we are not beautiful.

Despite these stereotypes that continue to shape the misconceptions of who we are today, our presence in society remains multifaceted and varied. We are short and tall, slender and wide-hipped, black, brown, and yellow. Our hair is kinky, curly, straight, braided, and up-doed. Black women are CEOs, entrepreneurs, office workers, chefs, educators, journalists, health-care professionals, and so much more. Despite what others believe, we know that we are not—and have never been—"one way."

In each chapter of this book, you will see a box labeled "Sister Circle Note." These inspirational affirmations are motivational notes to encourage you to take positive actions when dealing with stressful situations, and they give a positive scripture reference for further understanding and personal growth.

FORMING OUR RESPONSES TO ANGER IN THE CHILDHOOD YEARS

Our anger styles are often formed when we are young. Our anger expressions can be understood from how our parents expected us

---

SISTER CIRCLE NOTE #1

Start using a journal to write about why you're angry and what your needs are. Note your reactions to stressful events.

I know that God will supply all my needs!

READ PSALM 37:1–11

---

to behave. For example, Karla remembers acting out her anger at a very early age. "Mama would get angry with me and holler, 'Karla Ann, you pick up those cotton pickin' toys right now!' She always called me by my first and middle name when she was upset."

In turn, Karla, the eldest child, patterned her own anger style after her mother. She screamed loudly at her younger brother, "Junior, you give me my cotton pickin' ball right now." When Karla emulated her mother's behavior, her mother would chastise her and ask her "What did I hear you say?" Then she would threaten to whip her if she heard her say "cotton pickin' " again. Karla would become even angrier with her brother for smirking when she got in trouble. When Karla's mother turned her back, she would take the ball away from Junior, after her mother had told her to give it to him. Karla sought her own method of justice because she felt that her brother always had his way with Mama.

Karla also has vivid memories of her mother and father arguing bitterly. After Karla's dad came home, she would run to him and say, "Daddy, Mama hit me today." Her father would always side with his little girl and reprimand her mother, "I thought I told you not to put your hands on my kids?" Her mother's standard reaction was, "Last I knew, they were my kids, too; spare the rod, spoil the child." Her family would fight in anger triangles: first Karla, her brother, and her mother; then Karla, her mother, and her father. As an adult, if Karla has a disagreement with someone, she can't let a subject drop and she always involves a third party in her battles. She needs someone to join in on an issue, and she feels compelled to continue the argument.

Janice also modeled her anger after a parent. She does not remember acting out her anger as a child because her mother never permitted her to express "those types" of feelings. She was not allowed to "talk back" since it was considered disrespectful to do so with your parents. Janice's mother and father always told her to respond with "yes, ma'am" and "yes, sir." "Everytime my mother or father called and I said 'huh,' they would say 'excuse me?' And I would say, 'I mean yes, ma'am or sir.' I even referred to my friends' parents the same way and some of the kids would laugh at me and tell me that I sounded so country when I talked like that. We lived in New York but my folks were from down South. That's the way folk down South spoke. It was proper." Part of what Janice's parents considered obedience also included a lack of facial expression. Janice was not allowed to look upset when her parents fussed at her. If she was caught rolling her eyes, huffing and puffing, or stomping, she could expect a whipping.

Her father encouraged different emotional responses for his daughter and son. Her older brother was free to become angry and exhibit aggressive behavior. Janice remembers her father telling her brother that if he came home crying from a fight he would whip him. As she was growing up, Janice often experienced anxiety attacks, especially when others around her disagreed. She would apologize for things she hadn't even done. Since she was not allowed to experience anger as a child, Janice learned to internalize her feelings. Now an adult, she avoids confrontation and expresses anger only as a reaction; she walks away instead of facing an argument.

Think about how you handle your anger and what you learned as a child about expressing emotions. After witnessing an angry encounter between adults, or anger expressed directly toward you, did an adult offer an explanation to ease your fears?

DEALING WITH ANGER EXPLOSIVELY CREATES A DANGEROUS CYCLE

Susan was trapped in harmful patterns with her boyfriend Skip. Skip would stay out late and return home smelling like alcohol, or not make it in until the wee hours of the morning. When Susan would ask him where he had been, he would tell her "out" and to "stop trying to control him." Susan would go off sapphire style. Skip would physically abuse her. In response to her angry outbursts and his guilt for hitting her, Skip would cry and apologize. These ugly scenes were the only times that Susan had Skip's full attention and cooperation. Finally, Susan began therapy because she needed someone to talk to about the situation and she was too embarrassed to discuss it with friends.

At first, Susan really believed that blindly going off was the answer to her problems with Skip, but with the help of therapy she began to see things differently. She realized that she was deeply angry, but she felt guilt and anxiety for lashing out so furiously at someone she thought she loved. As soon as she recognized that going off allowed her to justify maintaining a relationship that she was afraid to let go of, Susan told Skip that she could not date him until he sought counseling for his problem. Going off contributed to Susan's emotional turmoil and placed her at risk for a cyclic pattern of abuse with her boyfriend.

From Susan's story, we can see how going off can be the tip of an iceberg of anger. Going off without thinking through situations distracts us from the real issues at hand. Generally, when we explode in this way, it's because we are frightened and we do not have the ability to cope. We use the process of venting to create space between ourselves and our fear, numbing ourselves in the process, and often alienating others. We often feel guilty after losing control, so we repress our unresolved feelings in order to punish ourselves for this loss of control. Such behavior, of course, leads to further complications and misery. If we continue to hide our anger to avoid expressing it, we may find ourselves suffering from the Invincible Black Woman syndrome, a condition that sisters experience when they want to maintain the appearance of staying strong by placing themselves last despite their feelings.

WHY MEN HATE TO SEE SISTAS ANGRY

When we asked men about black women and anger, they defensively wanted to know if *Going Off* is going to make suggestions for sistas to take their anger out on men. Why? Because when we talk about going off we talk about our heartaches, bodies, children, and dreams, which often involve our men.

Picture this fantasy: the man whom you've been waiting to call finally gives you a ring. He apologizes for not keeping in touch over the past few days. He tells you he'll be right over to talk with you and he'll bring take out with him so the two of you can chat over dinner. He asks you if you need anything from the store while he's on his way. He arrives at your place and he looks into your eyes and says, "Baby, what's wrong? Are you angry?" You look at him and become emotional, ready to cry, ready to talk.

Oops, this is just a fantasy. Most men are not ready for this type of candid conversation. Usually, when women get angry, men are oblivious to the cause of their anger. Men seem completely unaware of what sisters are going through. To talk about women's anger threatens them because they feel they might be asked to change, and they are happy with things as they are. In the fantasy we just related, the sista felt put out by waiting for him to call and she was tired of trying to decipher where the relationship was heading. She thought he should understand her feelings without her having to explain them, a common feeling of sisters with the Invincible Black Woman syndrome, and she thought he should offer an explanation for his behavior. From his point of view, everything was fine. As far as he could tell, she had no reason to be angry. Besides, she always told him how happy she was whenever they spent time together.

DISCUSS RESENTMENTS OPENLY

Rose agreed to stay home and rear the children but she often felt isolated and lonely. She wanted to return to the career she had left, but she knew that her husband, Jay, was against it. Since Jay enjoyed his career and success, and expected his wife to feel privileged to stay at home, any general "what if" discussions about the situation were canned. It became a daily routine for Jay to come home from work in inspector mode looking around the house, complaining about something that Rose didn't do. Rose began to harbor anger and feel a growing resentment toward Jay. She called her previous co-workers in order to keep in touch with the work world. She realized with chagrin that her responsibilities changed from handling accounts for a finance company to counting how much money her husband had left her for lunch and cleaning the house. Jay avoided addressing the issue because ignoring Rose's anger allowed him to travel on his job and continue his career advancement.

Often, sisters are pressured not to ask for change from men. If a sister expresses her anger openly, she is told that her behavior isn't ladylike. Sometimes she is labeled "ungrateful." Many sisters have grown up with confused and suppressed feelings of anger that began with early encouragement from their parents to show "ladylike behavior." Do you know how early conditioning has affected the way you respond when angry? How were you allowed to express your anger? What happened after you displayed your anger?

COMPLETE THE BLACK Woman's Anger Quotient test on the following page to understand more clearly where you are in your ability to assess your level of frustration tolerance. There are no right or wrong answers. Answer according to how you initially respond.

THE BLACK WOMAN'S ANGER QUOTIENT (AQ)

1. You become extremely annoyed if a driver cuts you off and takes the parking space that you intended to use.

   a) Usually   **b)** Sometimes   **c)** Rarely

2. You become agitated if you are next in line and are overlooked by a salesperson.

   a) Usually   **b)** Sometimes   **c)** Rarely

3. You feel angry and frustrated when the grocery store line moves slowly.

   a) Usually   **b)** Sometimes   **c)** Rarely

4. You become defensive and confrontational if you learn that gossip has been spread about you.

   a) Usually   **b)** Sometimes   **c)** Rarely

5. You become extremely agitated if a salesperson follows you around a store for no helpful reason.

   a) Usually   **b)** Sometimes   **c)** Rarely

6. You become irritated and defensive when a supervisor criticizes your work in front of co-workers.

   a) Usually   **b)** Sometimes   **c)** Rarely

7. When cashing a check, you become agitated if a bank teller acts suspiciously.

   a) Usually   **b)** Sometimes   **c)** Rarely

8. You are appalled and angry when you discover a confidential matter has been leaked.

   a) Usually   **b)** Sometimes   **c)** Rarely

9. When you pick up fast food, you become aggravated when you get home and discover that you have been given the wrong order.

   a) Usually   b) Sometimes   c) Rarely

10. You are angry and annoyed when watching television or movies or reading books that portray stereotypical images of African Americans.

    a) Usually   b) Sometimes   c) Rarely

SCORING:
Each "A" Answer = 0 Points
Each "B" Answer = 1 Point
Each "C" Answer = 2 Points

0–6 Points: (Low AQ) You have low tolerance and need to become aware of anger triggers. You also need to get in touch with your feelings about anger and how you respond to them.

7–14 Points: (Average AQ) You are in the middle range of frustration tolerance. Work on your awareness of your feelings about anger and your anger triggers.

15–20 Points: (High AQ) You have excellent tolerance for frustration. However, stay in touch with your feelings about anger and become aware of the Invincible Black Woman syndrome in case you have a defense system that denies anger until you experience something so powerful that you explode.

INTERNALIZING ANGER LEAVES US POWERLESS

As we mentioned earlier, anger manifests itself in countless ways. Generally speaking, anger is either directed outward or it is internalized. During a women and anger workshop, Ann had little to say about her anger. She was not an active workshop participant, but whenever one of the sisters made eye contact with her, she simply smiled while others shared serious moments about their feelings of anger. Following the workshop, Ann decided to schedule a therapy session. She had quite a lot to be angry about. Ann was pregnant, and her husband, who had a drug problem, had recently left in the middle of the night. When she woke up one morning, she found that the cash in the house was gone, and she was left penniless with a toddler to care for. Throughout most of the workshop, Ann had sat apart from the other women. Masking her emotions by smiling, Ann did not participate because she did not want the other women in the group to know the truth about her situation.

When Ann and her husband had been together, he dominated her. When he left her, Ann didn't know how to express her anger and displeasure at what he had done to her and their relationship; so instead of openly dealing with this anger, she internalized her frustration.

WE SOMETIMES VIEW anger as something that we need to stop, hide, control, and avoid, regarding it as an emotion we shouldn't use. Some of us try to keep our secret, thinking, "I can't let them see me become angry. They've never seen me this way before." When we attempt to hide our anger, we begin to harm ourselves and start to fall into the Invincible Black Woman syndrome.

2 THE INVINCIBLE BLACK WOMAN SYNDROME

"It would be nice to have some room for emotional flexibility, but then we don't have a clue as to what emotional stability looks like for ourselves."

—JULIA BOYD, *IN THE COMPANY OF MY SISTERS*

THE INVINCIBLE BLACK WOMAN (IBW) syndrome tells us to ignore or deny our anger, carry self-imposed burdens, and remain strong all of the time. This creates difficulty in managing our limitations or weaknesses. It also mistakenly tells us that other people should recognize our weaknesses without being told, such as feeling beaten by a hard day at work and coming home to cook when we really don't feel like cooking. We feel our spouse should take us out to a nice place to eat, without us having to ask. The IBW syndrome leads us to maintain a strong front all the time, not look at or discuss our weaknesses, and when we need help, expect someone to know that and help us for all that we do. When we remain silent about our needs, we sometimes get fed up and go off.

The IBW syndrome also fools us into thinking that no one can fill in for us and help get the job done, so we should just do it ourselves. This syndrome leads us to believe that we can add more and more to our plate because we are strong and we can do it. It encourages us to take crap all day at work and bring more work home with us. It compels us to accept all requests for favors and never say no without guilt. The IBW syndrome can make us ill, give us headaches, cause our blood pressure to rise, and contribute to overeating. Basically, the IBW syndrome stems from the desire to please. Let's examine how the IBW syndrome affects women in their lives.

HOW SELF-NEGLECT LEADS TO ANGER

Ali, a retail salesperson, married at a young age. Although she had dreams of becoming a professional singer, she took low wage jobs so that her husband could finish college; she felt it was her responsibility to support his career goals. Ali postponed an opportunity to take special music instruction because she felt the money would be better spent on items the children needed. At the time, she felt that the sacrifice was necessary.

Ali truly loved her husband and children, but she felt unappreciated and taken for granted most of the time. Due to these feelings, she often felt angry and bitter, and sometimes even unloved. She didn't share these feelings with her husband and children, but she sometimes became furious with them and exploded into anger for something that didn't warrant that kind of reaction.

When Ali exhibited this behavior, her family wouldn't know where it was coming from. And when she dished it out, she most likely received it in return. Her behavior didn't get her what she wanted at all. When Ali yelled at her children, they became more disagreeable and her husband would leave the house slamming the door, not wanting to deal with her when she acted this way.

As Ali's children grew up, she began to feel suffocated and

SISTER CIRCLE NOTE #2

Strong women are positive forces in our lives. Do something special today for a woman who has been a strong positive force in your life, or someone you may have taken for granted because she appears to have herself together. For the woman who has everything, perhaps a special handwritten note about something that she has done to help you will be appreciated.

I will use my talents wisely and my work will be blessed.

READ PROVERBS 31:29–31

wanted to change her life completely. She wanted to focus on her career and form a gospel singing group. Ali dreamed of performing before crowds and hearing the applause and admiration for her singing that she felt she so richly deserved.

Although Ali longed to achieve her goal of becoming a professional singer, she didn't openly share her disappointment with her family. However, she did let her family know how much they "got on her nerves." Sometimes Ali was so frustrated with her situation that she felt she couldn't take it another minute. She would complain to her husband about her feelings: "I've been standing on my feet waiting on people in stores for the last fifteen years—and then I come home and wait on people and I'm sick of it. No one does a thing around this house besides me. The next time I have to ask you to fix something around here and you don't fix it, I'm going to quit doing anything around here, too." Ali would also complain to her children: "Y'all get on my last nerve—you don't appreciate anything I do around here. The next time I come into the kitchen and it's dirty, I'm not cooking you anything to eat. I don't care if you're starving."

This pattern of negative complaining and going off didn't help Ali's family to understand her needs. She didn't receive any more respect or consideration from the family or any encouragement to pursue a singing career. No matter how much Ali complained, she continued to take care of everyone in the family and neglect her needs. Through her self-neglect she became angry and depressed.

When we fall into a role of caring for others as if it is expected of us, we often forget to care for ourselves. Since we don't expect it, we don't get it; and that makes us feel unappreciated and unhappy. Yet, despite these feelings of unhappiness, we remain silent, not requesting anything for ourselves from our mates or our children for fear of disappointing them. Sisters must understand that it is acceptable to request and receive love, and other things as well.

ACKNOWLEDGING WEAKNESS

Some sisters go off when they find themselves exhausted from the burden of being strong all the time. They feel like they've failed when they don't live up to others' expectations of a strong woman. Consider the case of Dianna Green, a prominent businesswoman, senior vice president at Duquesne Light Company, and civic leader in Pittsburgh. After she committed suicide, the account of her life in the *Wall Street Journal* described her as "one who cared most for others." In many ways, Green typified the Invincible Black Woman syndrome. After receiving national recognition in business, she suffered a series of unfortunate losses that she handled without complaint. However, when an investigation led to the disclosure that she had fabricated an MBA on her résumé, Green was forced to resign from her position at Duquesne. The humiliation, following so closely after other personal problems, proved to be too much and she took her own life. On the bottom of one of the attorneys' letters, Green noted in handwriting, "Thank you for making my last days on earth a living hell." Everyone who knew Dianna as a strong woman could not believe she lost control over her job. Dianna's crisis typified the Invincible Black Woman syndrome because she had difficulty balancing her weaknesses with her strengths. Weaknesses were too difficult to acknowledge.

Rebecca, a single parent, wrote a letter about her experiences of trying to present herself as an extremely strong, proud woman. The final blow for Rebecca came when her boyfriend left her for a former lover. His explanation to her was, "You're strong, Rebecca; you'll be okay. She needs me." Rebecca commented, "All my life I've been called strong. 'You're tough, Rebecca,' everyone said to me. 'You're a fighter.' This was even as a child. How strong is a child supposed to be? As I grew up, it seemed to me that only weak people cried out for help. I was married once; my husband was a Nigerian. He abandoned me and my young son to return to Nigeria. I was afraid to sue him for child support because I thought he might kidnap my son; consequently, I raised my son alone with no financial assistance."

THE SUPERWOMAN

The term "superwoman" became popular during the eighties when women began to manage both the household and careers outside the home. The superwoman was the woman who could do everything: make the money, prepare the food, clean and run the house, bear and raise the children, and please the husband in bed. The superwoman was always capable in any situation.

Phyllis had to experience a nervous breakdown before she was finally able to say no. At the design firm where she worked, she selected projects that she felt would move her up the ladder toward her goal of vice president. She often volunteered for additional assignments if another project in the office needed help, and she never said no if asked to take on any other task. Not surprisingly, Phyllis experienced a lot of personal anxiety and was often unable to sleep at night. Unexpected delays or projects that didn't work deeply affected Phyllis's self-esteem and brought feelings of fatigue and deep depression. Phyllis never recognized that the strong front that she created for herself was leading her to a complete collapse.

Janet had four children ages twelve to eighteen. She was proud of the fact that she had exceptional children and she built her world around them. Their interests were her interests. Janet spent her time going to cheerleading practice, football practice, Little League games, and the mall. She chauffeured the children and their friends to all their activities and she was proud of the fact that she was known as the "cool" mom. She worked two jobs to provide for her kids and loved it when she could provide her children with expensive sports equipment and designer clothes.

There were times when running back and forth became cumbersome, but now the kids were accustomed to getting everything they wanted and Janet found it impossible to tell them that she needed some rest before reporting to her second job. The more money Janet spent on her kids, the less it seemed to her that they appreciated it. Janet couldn't remember the last time she refused one of her children's requests. It was frustrating for her to work so hard and see new items of clothing or toys that she bought for the kids thrown carelessly on the floor.

Janet's children became more demanding and less appreciative for the sacrifices that she made for them. She began to worry about her physical stamina. Janet felt that if she went to another football game, dance rehearsal, or soccer practice that she would suffer from a breakdown, but she continued to do so because she didn't want to lose her "cool mom" title. Janet started to notice that her hair began to fall out but her doctor said that it was her "nerves" and started her on a medication to treat anxiety. He also recommended that she see a psychotherapist. "Per my doctor's orders I decided to see a counselor to help me figure out what I could do about my relationship with the kids."

Everyone experiences feelings of vulnerability and helplessness. These feelings make us doubt our ability to do a good job at work or to be a good mother, daughter, sister, or student. We can gain perspective if we accept the fact that we all experience feelings of self-doubt from time to time. Becoming aware of our strengths will also help. Falling into the Invincible Black Woman syndrome by denying our natural feelings of vulnerability, and believing that we are the mythical superwoman who can do it all, can lead us to internalized anger and depression.

CHARACTERISTICS OF THE INVINCIBLE BLACK WOMAN SYNDROME

Through our research, and countless interviews with women, we have identified the major characteristics of the Invincible Black Woman syndrome. We not only interviewed women, but we also interviewed men. Women that we interviewed viewed their strengths as a positive. However, in many instances they were afraid to admit to weaknesses about situations that seemed out of their control. These women wanted to please others, but felt victimized because they thought people would take advantage of them and never return the favor. Men that we interviewed, who identified their mates as strong women, spoke of the perplexity of admiring the strength in their women but had difficulty understanding when their strong-willed women would cry out of the blue or go off without provocation. By this, men described women who would go off the deep end and tell them about things that happened a long time ago. By the time women mentioned these complaints, the details were fuzzy and the men didn't recall the situation with nearly as much detail, nor did they have a clue that their mate was intensely upset about the event. There is nothing wrong with displaying frustrations, crying, or expressing anger, but when it's taken to an extreme it's debilitating.

Denial

A woman in denial has difficulty saying "no" because she thinks of herself as a superwoman able to assist others regardless of what else she needs to do. Even when drained or depleted, she makes herself available for others. The Invincible Black Woman cannot say no to family requests, social activities, or invitations, even if she does not have the time and energy for such things. Always saying "yes" contributes to her personal anxiety.

Low Self-Esteem

Often women don't receive the encouragement they need as they grow up. These women have acquired negative self-talk that contributes to low self-esteem. Women who completely go off after some form of rejection usually have a problem with low self-esteem, and they lose control because they thought that they were strong and could handle the situation. When women maintain a strong front, it usually means that they have a hard time seeing or accepting themselves as they really are. Usually, they do this in order to live up to others' expectations. Depending upon others to validate their self-worth can leave them with a sense of powerlessness that increases low self-esteem.

Getting Involved in Others' Problems

In the caretaker role, the Invincible Black Woman often becomes involved with other people's problems, or she attempts to rescue others from their problems. People find such women easy to confide in. These women are good listeners and can serve as confidantes for others. However, in taking on others' problems, they actually try to solve them. They become more deeply involved and begin to live other people's problems in the form of secondary stress. Women with this characteristic exhaust themselves with their futile efforts in solving others' problems.

Workaholic Tendencies

Strong women with workaholic tendencies overextend themselves and take on too many tasks, many of which do not necessarily fulfill them. These women have difficulty sorting through their priorities. They accept too many projects at once. They correlate their identity with their work. In this pattern of working, they can find themselves in over their heads. Women with workaholic tendencies expect too much from themselves, they make commitments that aren't physically possible to fulfill, and they find themselves in a constant state of anxiety because they think they are not accomplishing as much as they should. While these qualities may appear admirable, they are an open invitation to failure.

Depression

When the Invincible Black Woman fails to meet her own expectations, the feelings of loss and disappointment can result in a painful depression. Interestingly enough, not all women can recognize when they are depressed. One woman may experience symptoms such as crying spells and listlessness, while another will smile and deny that anything is wrong. "I was snapping at everyone—anything someone said set me off. I was depressed and I didn't know it," a survey respondent disclosed. Some women eat and sleep too much, while others lose their appetite and complain of insomnia. Some women may not feel depressed, but they experience depression as a loss of interest or pleasure in their activities, including sex. Sometimes you hear women say, "I've given up on men," or "I've given up on sex."

PHASES OF THE INVINCIBLE BLACK WOMAN SYNDROME

There is no shame in admitting that we cannot do everything. We need to understand that even the strongest women will turn vulnerable under the weight of unreasonable expectations. We must learn to know our own limitations and see that it is okay to ask for help or to accept assistance from others. We don't have to do everything ourselves, and we don't have to handle things alone. Acknowledging our weaknesses will not make us powerless. Power doesn't come from putting up a strong front.

The Invincible Black Woman syndrome can be broken down into beginning, middle, and end phases. Each phase grows progressively worse as the following examples will show.

The Beginning Phase: Seeking Approval

Sharon, voted most likely to succeed by her high school senior class, readily admitted to having a people-pleaser personality. The bright, cheerful, optimistic cheerleader had set goals for college and a career; however, she got pregnant right after graduation. Giving in to feelings of insecurity, Sharon worried what others would think of her pregnancy and her good girl image. Even though there was no indication that the baby's father might be "Mr. Right," Sharon married him a year later because she felt it was virtuous to marry the father of her child. Sharon put her misgivings aside, and in doing so, she showed early symptoms of the Invincible Black Woman syndrome.

In true Invincible Black Woman style, Sharon began to grow overly concerned with how others perceived her. Seeking ap-

proval from everyone, she validated her worth through the reactions she received from others. The Invincible Black Woman
syndrome progressed further because, as Sharon increasingly
made decisions about the baby, her marriage, and work based on
fearing a loss of approval, she denied her real feelings.

HAVE YOUR EVER done something with what you thought were
good motivations only to find disastrous results? "Why did I do
this?" you ask in horror and surprise. It is almost guaranteed
that if you re-examine your actions in such a situation, you will
see that fear lies at the heart of the matter. Fear of how you
will look if you lose your man; fear of what people will think if
you are single and pregnant; working at a job you absolutely
deplore because of the fear that you aren't capable of doing
anything else. If you can see yourself in these examples, then it
is possible that you suffer from the Invincible Black Woman
syndrome.

Basic Fears

Many women are overly concerned with what others think about
them. They spend an unnecessary and exaggerated amount of
time trying to live up to others' demands and expectations. They
lack self-confidence and cannot set reasonable goals for themselves. Such women direct themselves outward, seeking affirmation from others instead of developing their inner qualities.
Feeling fragile and vulnerable because their happiness and validation of self-worth depends on others, women who live this way
are plagued with feelings of self-doubt and failure. There are
countless causes for such low self-esteem, all of which appear to
stem from fear.

INVINCIBLE BLACK WOMAN SYNDROME SCALE

INTENSITY

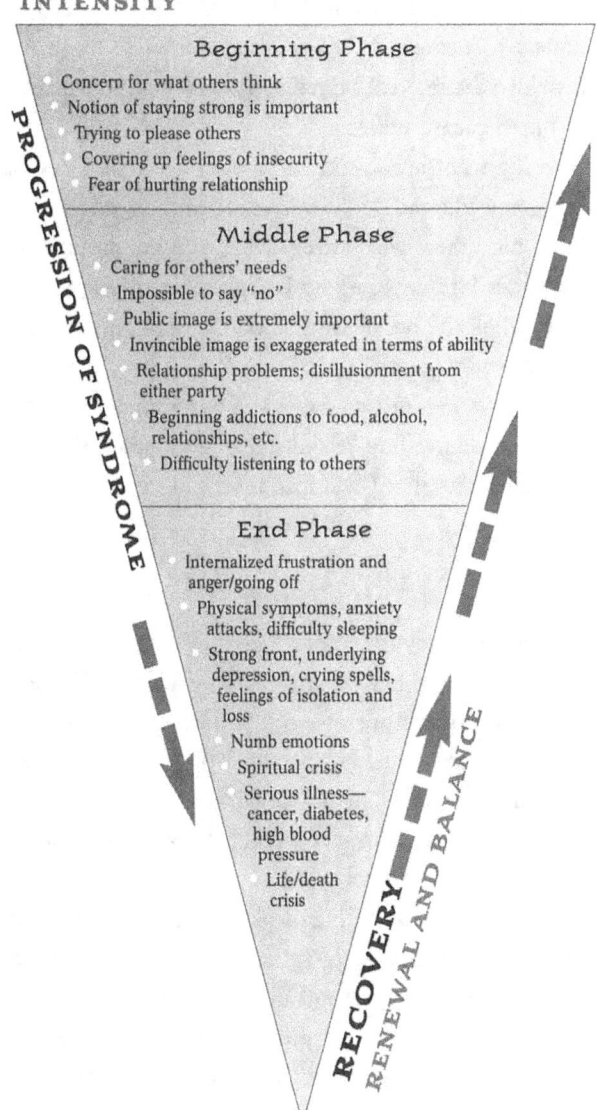

Beginning Phase

- Concern for what others think
- Notion of staying strong is important
- Trying to please others
- Covering up feelings of insecurity
- Fear of hurting relationship

Middle Phase

- Caring for others' needs
- Impossible to say "no"
- Public image is extremely important
- Invincible image is exaggerated in terms of ability
- Relationship problems; disillusionment from either party
- Beginning addictions to food, alcohol, relationships, etc.
- Difficulty listening to others

End Phase

- Internalized frustration and anger/going off
- Physical symptoms, anxiety attacks, difficulty sleeping
- Strong front, underlying depression, crying spells, feelings of isolation and loss
- Numb emotions
- Spiritual crisis
- Serious illness— cancer, diabetes, high blood pressure
- Life/death crisis

PROGRESSION OF SYNDROME

RECOVERY

RENEWAL AND BALANCE

- **Fear of appearing weak translates into the notion of staying strong.**

  "I must be there for him," "I can't ask him to repay the money he borrowed."
- **Fear that others will be unhappy with you translates into trying to please others.**

  "I really want her to like me. I can't be myself because she might not like me."
- **Fear that others will perceive that you are not in control translates into covering up feelings of insecurity.**

  "Out of all the people in this office, I am the only one who can follow through."
- **Fear of the loss of love from a spouse, family member, or friend translates into fear of hurting a relationship.**

  "I'm so afraid that I will lose him, so I had better dress the way he likes."

Self-Doubt

Courtney had a successful career, yet she derived her feelings of success from the way her co-workers viewed her. If there were problems or confrontations at work, Courtney suffered from depression and perceived herself, instead of her co-workers, as ineffective. For example, Courtney fought hard to win presidency of a local women's group and won. When questioned by a group of women within the organization about a problem that existed before she was even elected, Courtney took the criticism personally. The fact that the women might actually be trying to address a real issue in a workable way did not occur to Courtney. She saw the encounter as just another indication of her own failings. She felt threatened by the other women. Courtney was so vulnerable that she met any outside comments defensively. "I thought those women were my friends," she cried bitterly. "Now I see that they are out to get me."

Sarah also relied heavily on others' perceptions. She grew up with a mother who lived her entire life viewing herself through the eyes of others. Her mother was unable to make decisions and never felt that she measured up to anyone else. "I was in college and my roommate turned to me and said, 'You know, Sara, you're really a smart and pretty girl. Why don't you think so?' I realized that I had always doubted my looks, my grades—nearly everything. I had learned my mother's behavior and I was carrying those same low self-esteem issues that she did."

The Middle Phase: Trouble Saying No

Women in the middle phase of the Invincible Black Woman syndrome are afraid to let someone know that they need help or that they have limitations. They frequently take on much more than they can handle because they refuse to admit that they have taken on too much, or because they don't want to cause hurt feelings. Silence about their feelings, hurt, and self-blame leads to addictions to food, alcohol, and dependent relationships.

Regina was trying to do all the housework, work outside the home, take care of her two kids, and assist her elderly parents. She was silent and resentful about her situation; she felt that her whole life revolved around caring for others' needs. She would become angriest when she pushed herself to prepare a special meal that turned out to be unappreciated by her family. She would smile on the outside, but she felt like crying because there was never enough time to take care of everything. When her elderly parents needed more help and assistance from her, she felt as if they didn't understand how busy she was. Regina put on her best face in front of her friends telling them that she had the best of both worlds, her husband was a good provider and she had the perfect family. However, she felt pressure from all of her responsibilities.

Regina hates confrontation and has trouble saying no, thus she sends mixed messages to her children; she gives in to them but uses body language to show she really disapproves of them. Since she rarely tells them no, she raises the children with a very permissive hand.

Regina's children are not only confused by the mixed signals she sends, they are often perceived as spoiled brats. Frequently, Regina's elderly parents ask for her assistance and she always responds. When her husband leaves the house and refuses to give her an explanation about where he is going, her eyes narrow, her lips purse, and you can visibly see her face tighten. Regina says nothing, as if she is not bothered by this behavior but she usually develops a headache. Regina's friends know that her husband is not around often and offer their support, but she doesn't accept their offers and tells them that everything is okay. Then her friends secretly gossip with one another about her because they view her as phony, seeing through the strong front that Regina works hard to maintain. They know that the perfect family she pretends to have is false.

Women in phase two experience pressure to keep up an exaggerated strong image in terms of their ability to follow through. Often over-committed because they are unable to say no, these women place their public image above all else. This strong image is artificial and exaggerated, and it requires quite a bit of effort to maintain. Women who have experienced the middle phase of the syndrome often cite relationship problems as the cause, sometimes including difficulty listening to others.

The Last Phase: The Physical Symptoms of Internalized Anger

The last phase of the syndrome can send the body into such stress from internalized frustration and anger that women start exhibiting physical symptoms, such as anxiety attacks and difficulty sleeping. The National Cancer Institute reports that many types of stress activate the bio-endocrine immune system, which is the system that causes changes in the body's defense against infectious disease.

Rebecca, the single parent discussed earlier in this chapter, had been having anxiety attacks and at one point even thought that she was having a heart attack. But it was actually anger, frustration, and confusion. Everything around her was getting on her nerves. She didn't like making $15,000 a year. She didn't receive child support. Her son had asthma, and his hospital bills had soared from many emergency room visits. At one point, the hospital even refused to treat him. Even though Rebecca gave the hospital her financial information, the hospital sued her for the medical bills and obtained a judgment against her. When her boyfriend left her for a former lover, she decided she just couldn't get men to stick around. She thought that the men in her life had always viewed her as someone looking for a man to raise her son. That's when she fell into the final phase of the Invincible Black Woman syndrome. Rebecca felt that she had no one to talk to about her frustration and internalized her anger. She grew severely depressed and cried on and off for three days, and she developed anxiety attacks, symptoms of her internalized anger.

Sharon first got married because she feared what others would think of her as a young unwed mother. After marrying, she subsequently divorced, and was left with three boys to raise. Her ex-husband only provided sporadic support. She often worked two jobs to try to make up for what her children weren't getting. "I felt guilty that I could only be a mother to them and not both a mother and father," Sharon said. "I felt guilty that I had not chosen a better father for them." At the same time, she experienced internalized frustration and anger.

She remarried seven years later and that marriage also ended in divorce. "I thought that was it—a magical moment," Sharon said. "Both of us were in the church, so I figured we couldn't go wrong. It turned out to be the most devastating relationship of my life. When things would go wrong, I would talk to my minister and convince myself that if I stayed strong in the Lord everything would be all right." Friends and family thought of Sharon and her husband as a perfect couple because Sharon kept up such a strong front. Secretly, however, Sharon suffered from underlying depression with symptoms of crying spells, feelings of isolation and loss. Sharon's new husband was both verbally and physically abusive to her and her children. She developed a serious illness because she stopped eating. Her weight dropped to less than one hundred pounds, and her hair fell out. Eventually, her emotions became numb. She experienced a spiritual and life and death crisis. "Finally," Sharon said, "I contemplated suicide. Being strong was killing me." How women recover from the Invincible Black Woman syndrome is discussed in Part III of this book.

3 ANGER TRIGGERS

"Every time he said that I was 'overly emotional,' I
would lose it. Anyone who makes that comment
can expect trouble from me. I can't help it. It's my
trigger."

—PAM

EVERY WOMAN HAS TRIGGERS. In a way, they are
the wires that connect us with our past experiences of anger. A
trigger results from our ability to retain reaction or memory to
the stimuli of things that have happened to us. When a memory
is actually a trigger, we know it because each time we encounter
the stimulus we respond accordingly, as if we are wired or pro-
grammed to that response. With triggers, we have no time to think
things through. When we don't have time to think, we often behave stupidly while under the influence of triggers.

WHAT CAUSES OUR ANGER TRIGGERS?

Our triggers can provoke emotions that range from mild and
vague to strong and powerful. Triggers are always a problem, and
more important, they are an embarrassment. They can cause us
to appear illogical, out of control, immature, foolish, strange—

you name it. Sometimes our emotional responses to triggers are so powerful that we become verbally and physically aggressive. If you have ever reached this state, and you want to remove anger from your life, it is important to know mechanics that lie behind your trigger responses. Read through the following descriptions of common triggers and ask yourself which ones really set you off. Then, the next time you get angry, ask yourself, "Why am I responding in such a hostile manner? Where is this anger coming from?" Chapter 8 will help you identify and overcome your anger triggers.

Dissin' (Disrespect)

Due to our history in America, black women have always had to deal with issues of respect. Slave owners disrespected black women; it was common practice for them to have their way with any slave woman on the plantation.

When a black woman feels disrespected, or dissed, feelings of anger well up inside her. Remembering past and current struggles contributes to the anxiety felt when disrespected. After all, relationships with others are important to sisters, and we appreciate respect in these interactions.

Carolyn, a twenty-one-year-old bank teller who sought therapy, described her triggers. What set her off most was when somebody spoke disrespectfully to her. Carolyn had to appear in court after she physically attacked a girlfriend. "I remember she called me a bitch," Carolyn said. "I was angry, but when she started talking about my mother, I lost control. She didn't even know my mother."

When a sister is called the "b" word it is a trigger. The "b" word is considered disrespectful because it is associated with

meanness and unfeminine characteristics. We have been trained to act ladylike and the "b" word represents the exact opposite. Like many sisters, Carolyn feels that she is a nice person. So when her friend called her a bitch, it triggered anger because her friend insinuated that she was the opposite of what she had been trained to be, a kind sister who acts ladylike. When Carolyn was young, there were playground fights at her school. The rule was that you could say anything as long as you didn't talk about anyone's mother. Those were fighting words. Carolyn had been conditioned since childhood to feel that unsolicited negative comments about a parent are unacceptable and disrespectful. So before Carolyn knew what she was doing, she was physically attacking her friend. She still doesn't remember everything she did because she felt as if she blacked out when she started to hit her friend. After being fined in court, Carolyn finally decided to come to counseling to seek help with her anger.

Marilyn, an advertising executive, feels most disrespected when she does a favor for someone who subsequently forgets the favor. For example, Marilyn helped her client, Mr. Valentine, with an ailing used car business by putting together an advertising plan that increased sales by fifty percent. At the time, Mr. Valentine was desperate and grateful for Marilyn's expertise. Later, after the business recovered, Marilyn made a follow-up call to Mr. Valentine to review his need for advertising. She was unable to speak with Mr. Valentine, however, because he had his secretary tell Marilyn that he had just left the office. Marilyn felt most disrespected by his treatment because Mr. Valentine spoke through his secretary. She felt that he could at least have enough respect for her as a businesswoman to tell her directly that he was not interested in doing any advertising business with her. She then would have had an opportunity to explain the advantages of using her services and remind him that she had helped increase his business when it was failing. Marilyn grew flustered by the dishonesty of the situation, and she thought about reprimanding the secretary to remind her that she deserved respect. Instead of speaking to the secretary about the problem, however, she slammed down the phone when she hung up. She went into a rage and threw the phone across the room, knocking several treasured African statuettes off the mantle and they broke into a million pieces on the floor. Later when she had calmed down, she regretted both her loss of temper and loss of her precious African artifacts.

False Accusations

In the women and anger workshops, false accusations were cited as frequent triggers for anger. Black people have a history of being falsely accused, especially in the criminal justice system. Sisters related experiences of people watching them in places like retail stores when they browse around to look at items. For example Constance, a substitute teacher, said that a false accusation led security to attempt to arrest her for shoplifting at a mall. At the time, Constance had been seven months pregnant when she decided to go Easter shopping with her sister at a popular clothing store. Although Constance wasn't shopping for herself, she was helping her sister look for a dress to wear on Easter Sunday. Feeling tired, Constance told her sister that she was going to take a seat outside the store in the mall. While her sister shopped inside the store, Constance was approached by mall security and told to come back inside the store with them because the salesperson reported that Constance was stuffing clothes inside her pants where her pregnant belly was. Constance informed security that she was pregnant. Security refused to listen to her, took her into the back of the store, and examined her belly and her purse. They found nothing and allowed Constance to leave the store. Constance and her sister were very angry and they both went off sista sass style on the salesperson and the store manager.

Judy, a twenty-five-year-old supervisor for a social service agency, felt outraged and pressured to resign from her job because of false accusations. The daughter of a major donor joined the agency's staff and began to make life miserable for other employees as she attempted to gain power. She went to the boss with accusations that Judy and her co-workers were not doing their jobs, stating that volunteers and clients made complaints about them. As a supervisor, Judy began to investigate the complaints and discovered that they were untrue. But due to the status of the accuser, Judy's response to the accusations was futile. "After spending hours analyzing this mess and writing things down and looking for ways to understand my anger," Judy said, "I began to see that I have always detested dishonesty. But when lies are told by someone who rats on somebody else, that really makes me mad. When I was a kid, our parents made a big deal about what they called 'tattling.' I was punished by my parents for being a tattletale, so eventually I quit doing it; but now, as an adult when I see someone tattling, I get really mad. And when the whole thing is a lie, and it's about me, I have a hard time controlling myself."

False accusations are especially painful, leaving sisters feeling victimized, paranoid, and helpless. Far-reaching repercussions can result, such as being fired, fined by court, or even imprisoned. False accusations are not only anger triggers; they also can contribute to the development of a continuous state of anger. With

---

SISTER CIRCLE NOTE #3

Using your journal, write down some of your anger triggers and how you respond to them.

I know that in the face of adversity God is by my side.

READ PSALMS 27:12–14

---

no acceptable way to express their rage, some women suppress their feelings, go into denial, and develop the Invincible Black Woman syndrome.

Gwen was married to Frank, who was extremely jealous and insecure about their relationship. Gwen was faithful and had little jealousy herself, so she was especially impatient and intolerant of Frank's jealousy. She found it a waste of time and an insult to be accused of looking at other men. "He was destroying our marriage with his fears. He was so afraid that I'd find someone else that he developed a source of conflict that otherwise would not be there. Not only did he make me angry about all this, but it also hurt my feelings. I felt so frustrated and wounded. We'd go out to eat and have a good time. I'd dress up, try to look my best, have a good time, and he'd start. 'Who are you thinking about? Why did you smile at that guy?' It was really crazy. Sometimes I'd go home and cry, but most of the time I'd lose my temper, and we would fight."

Part of the anguish and pain involved in false accusations is the feeling that we have been treated unjustly. Victims of such treatment often need to have someone hear or agree with their side of the story. "When things were at their worst, I couldn't stop thinking about the injustice of my husband's accusations," Gwen said. "My thoughts would go around and around in my mind. I talked to my sister. I know she got sick of hearing me. I guess I became obsessed with talking about my problems, and it just didn't seem to me that I could solve them. I'm really grateful to my sister for being there for me."

Discrimination

Whether we are discriminated against because of our race, gender, or sexual orientation, standing at the receiving end of discrimination can cause feelings of anger and undeniable hurt. In the Jim Crow days of separate accommodations, our grandparents couldn't eat in white restaurants, use white restrooms, drink from white water fountains, or attend white schools. To help cope with this, it sometimes helps to remember that the person who discriminates against us may also have feelings of rage because we are different, and he or she may not have acknowledged any of this in his or her own life.

As women enter the workforce in increasing numbers and attempt to break through the glass ceiling of the corporate world, they experience gender discrimination. Black women and other minority women have to face a double-edged sword of race and gender discrimination. Sisters say that men tell them they are tired of hearing about the glass ceiling because there really isn't one anymore. The typical female response to this is that males might not be aware of the glass ceiling because they aren't the ones who are experiencing that type of discrimination. Women have been discriminated against in business; we are discriminated against because of our age and we have experienced unfair credit practices.

When we fight for our rights, we're derisively called feminists, a label that has come to be regarded negatively.

Even though modern American society makes an attempt to address the issue of cultural diversity, many people are not completely willing to try to understand and appreciate differences between individuals and groups of people. Many workshops on diversity are being held across the country, but after those workshops and programs are over, many of the participants return to environments where differences are not taken into account. There have been many marches against discriminatory practices—gay pride marches, marches of women and children, the Million Woman March, the Million Man March—the list goes on. Unfortunately, many of the marches evoke anger in people who don't believe in the marches' causes.

Renee works in the corporate world, and she has recently experienced discrimination in business for the first time. In making business appointments with men outside her company, she has encountered rudeness and resistance, which she attributes to the fact that she is a woman. Once during casual conversation with a male associate at her own company, she remarked that she had an infant at home, and the response was, "You should be at home with that kid." Having a hard time dealing with gender discrimination, Renee is now so angry that she doesn't know how to cope with her anger. She feels oppressed and overwhelmed by the attitudes of the male associates within her company and by those of her outside clients.

Brandy, a twenty-four-year-old college student attending a predominately white university, experienced discrimination from one of her college professors. She loved the subject of her management class and had the best ideas when they broke up into small groups for class presentations. But when she took her midterm essay she received a D. Brandy was devastated by her poor grade and discussed her results with her peers after class. Brandy discovered that everyone in her class received a B grade or better on the essay except for herself and a student from India, the only minority students in the class.

Brandy decided to work more closely with the A students and formed a study group with several of them, all white males. During one study night, the males were joking about the professor and one stated, "She's an easy lay and an easy A." Brandy was shocked by the statement and asked what they meant by that statement. One of the students confidentially told her that their professor had dated several students in her class and that she planned to throw a keg party for them at the end of the quarter. She was also informed by the student that the professor had made a negative comment about Brandy's braided hairstyle and said that she didn't like niggers or foreigners.

Brandy studied hard for the take-home final and wrote out most of the answers for her group. This time Brandy knew that she cinched the test because she studied with the A group, jointly found the correct answers, and wrote her essay answers with the study group. Brandy received her final grade, a D. She couldn't believe it. Brandy became irate after finding out that her study counterparts received As on the take-home final that Brandy prepared with the group. Brandy finally decided to speak to her professor about her grade. The quarter was over and Brandy discovered that her teacher had left town because she was a visiting professor. Brandy spoke to the dean of the college about her hard work and resulting grade and the dean informed her that she would have to write to the professor to see if she would change her grade. Furious about her grade and feeling hopeless about the possibility that her professor would change it, she became depressed. Brandy vows to speak up the next time that she feels that someone is discriminating against her because they don't like her braids or the color of her skin.

Change

Change is a constant factor in our personal and professional lives today. Although change is a part of our life, it can bring upheaval with it. "When everything is going well, why change?" We find ourselves asking, "Why change when it seems as if it will make a situation worse?" Change is a trigger, a signal that takes many sisters out of their comfort zone, reminding them that things will not always be the same.

Change can affect every aspect of our lives: our living situation, our job, our marriage, our health, and our relationships with others. A natural response for many women is to deny change. "No! This can't be happening to me!" we cry in disbelief. When the realization sets in, the next step is anger. Change can threaten our equilibrium, remove our safety net, and leave us with feelings of loss.

One autumn, Angie went to New York for the weekend. When she left home, her mother was fine. Naturally, Angie called her mother when she arrived in New York, but she didn't get an answer. When Angie returned home, she called her sister to ask her where her mother had been. Surprisingly, Angie's sister hadn't seen or talked to their mother either. When Angie and her sister went to their mother's house, fearing the worst, they found their mother dead. Angie was devastated when her mother died. After the initial shock, she became angry with her sister, and would go off over simple matters. Silently she blamed her sister for their mother's death because she didn't check on her while she was away. Angie was extremely close to her mother and regarded her as her best friend. Angie misses her mother intensely, and she's angry because she just was not ready for this change in her life.

Mary Ann thought she would follow her husband, Neil, to the ends of the earth out of her love for him. During the course of their marriage, they moved from Michigan to Illinois, then to Ohio. Just as soon as Mary Ann felt settled in Ohio, however, Neil wanted her to move to Florida to be near her parents, while he moved to California. At first Mary Ann couldn't believe Neil was serious after what she had already been through. Then she became furious when she realized that he was serious. She couldn't believe that he wanted to consider a bicoastal marriage. This change evoked so much rage that Mary Ann became depressed and sought counseling. "When I married Neil," she said, "I made the most money, and he was struggling. I wanted to help him feel better about himself, so I let him uproot me three times. Now, I'm left alone while he makes his next move without me. I wonder if this time his moving without me is an excuse to have a relationship with another woman."

Mary Ann underwent several therapy sessions, and eventually she convinced Neil to attend one with her. During counseling, the couple professed love for one another, but expressed different viewpoints about the change Neil was introducing into their marriage. Neil saw the move as a wonderful career opportunity for him, but he felt that his travel schedule would force him to leave Mary Ann much of the time if she lived in California. In Florida, she would at least be near her parents. Mary Ann, on the other hand, saw the move as a devastating blow to their marriage. She suspected that Neil wanted to carry on an affair. What made her more angry was the fact that she had practically given up a successful career by following his career and moving from state to state over the past five years. Mary Ann's husband relocated to California without her, and Mary Ann filed for divorce.

Betrayal

Betrayal, an ultimate anger trigger, can be defined as "a complete let down by someone we trust." In such situations, we feel devastated. We are left alone without the relationship or friendship that we had counted on.

Women especially value relationships. Betrayal that results from the break-up of a relationship is often cited as a powerful anger trigger. In Patti LaBelle's autobiography, *Don't Block the Blessings,* she reveals feeling betrayed when a member of her singing group, The Bluebelles, left them for the Supremes. "Sara, Nina, and I were the last to get the word. It felt like someone put a knife in my heart. At first I was hurt, but then I got pissed."

Heather, a computer programmer and successfully employed professional, said that her anger was triggered by someone she had considered to be a good friend. The friend, who was also a roommate, constantly pointed out the flaws she saw in Tom, Heather's boyfriend. Eventually, Heather was influenced by the roommate's gossip and began to view Tom in a negative light. After Heather began to break up with Tom, her roommate started sleeping with him. She wasn't discreet about it either, saying that friends should confide everything in one another. Heather views herself as foolish for listening to her old roommate, but she also feels angry and perplexed by what she has come to regard as a betrayal by someone she considered a friend.

Crowds

Pushing and shoving in crowds are certainly anger triggers, as is someone jumping in front of you in line. Crowds can also pose danger; there have been casualties at concerts and sport events because of lack of crowd control. Even a Saturday trip to the mall can become stressful, especially with small children in tow. And just try to deal with getting the most popular toy around the holidays. Even going out to dinner on a Friday night can turn into a competitive and stressful event instead of a time for relaxing. The decision about where to go is the first issue; parking is then a problem; and inside the restaurant we are forced to wait for nearly an hour before we are seated. Dealing with crowds often becomes a major issue for families as they rush around trying to reward themselves with dining and entertainment.

Ruby went to Disney World with her family and the trip began to turn sour because of the crowd. The rides that they wanted to get on were at least a forty-five-minute to one-hour wait. Since the family traveled five hundred miles to get there they decided to wait in line. Ruby and her family waited to get on a ride and a man came and stood near them. Soon there was an entire family attempting to nonchalantly stand very close to them and move up in the line with them. Immediately after noticing what they were up to, Ruby went off on them and told them that she had been standing there for forty-five minutes and that they were not getting in front of her. A few others in the line made comments and the family walked away. Later, Ruby thought about the incident and figured that the family was not from the U.S. because they acted like they didn't understand English and perhaps didn't know that it was considered rude to jump the line.

Road Rage

When we are behind the wheel of a car, anger triggers can fire faster than at any other time. Stressed and hostile drivers who perceive some real or imagined threat from another driver engage in dangerous speeding, run-off-the-road passing, tailgating, and in some cases, physical violence and manslaughter. Traffic congestion is often the trigger for road rage.

Road rage is one of the fastest growing menaces on the highways today. According to an AAA Foundation for Traffic Safety survey, there has been a fifty-one percent increase in violent highway incidents since 1990. The survey indicates that nearly 13,000 people have been reported injured or killed in aggressive driving accidents since 1990. Attacking fellow drivers with guns, mace, and other weapons and engaging in demolition-derby tactics are some of the examples reported. Many aggressive driving incidents are never reported. Although the greater percentage of aggressive drivers are male, women must stay keenly aware of their triggers and responses to these aggressive drivers.

Women, along with children and the elderly, are often the victims of road rage. We must be careful not to allow our children to distract us as we drive. Something so simple as a lapse in attention may cause us to drive more slowly than normal or to cut someone off without realizing it. These things may set off an angry, aggressive driver. If we women join in the confrontation when our anger is triggered, we are at risk for attack. Something as harmless as honking our horn or giving a stern look can provoke violence.

Dionne was driving her sister home around 10:00 P.M. She noticed there was a driver tailgating her in an old racing car. She became angry and told her sister that she wanted that car off her bumper. She put on the brakes in the hope that the driver would get the message and stop tailgating her, but the driver only tail-gated her more closely than before. Every time she turned a cor-ner, the car behind her turned the corner. As they approached her sister's home, Dionne did not stop because she was afraid that the driver of the car would pull in too and try to harm them. Most of the stores in the neighborhood were closed, and the women were trying to think of where they could go for protection, but they didn't know where the nearest police station was located. They noticed the lights were still on at Burger King, so they pulled into the parking lot, but the car that was following them pulled in, too. Burger King was closed, but the employees had not left, so they went through the drive-in line, stopping to speak to the employees to ask for help. At that point, the driver stopped fol-lowing them and pulled away from the parking lot. Dionne and her sister made it home safely, but felt extremely nervous about the event.

Wanda was angry because her daughter forgot to pick up the milk when she went to the grocery store, so she slipped on some clothes and drove to the neighborhood store to pick up the milk herself. She saw a parking space near the door, but just as she was about to pull into the space a car zipped in ahead of her. She saw red. Wanda yelled at the woman and told her that she must have seen her getting ready to pull into that space. With equal indignation, the other woman denied seeing Wanda. Both women got out of their cars and continued yelling until the confrontation turned into a pushing and shoving match. The store manager called the police, and both women were nearly arrested.

Marsha loves to talk on her cell phone while driving in her car. She used to have difficulty concentrating on driving while on the phone, but now she feels it does not affect her ability to drive.

On workday mornings, she checks her voice mail while driving to work. One particular morning, she was listening to her voice mail with her head half cocked to one side, holding the phone to her ear. Marsha glanced in her rearview mirror and saw a man in the car behind her mouthing words at her. When Marsha put on her left turn signal to cross lanes, the driver behind her attempted to swerve around her, but Marsha beat him to the next lane. The aggravated driver then made a series of lane crossings, yelled at Marsha through the car window, wove in and out of traffic, and almost caused an accident. The actions of the other driver shocked Marsha. Growing nervous, wondering how far this angry driver might go to get her attention, she made a quick exit to lose him. The last she saw of him was in her rearview mirror as he gestured obscenely.

While browsing the Internet, Faye came across an angry letter from a man who stated that women should have special drivers' tests that include putting on makeup while driving and looking at children in the back seat. Knowing that this is a common attitude towards women, we should keep in mind how important it is to stay alert and defensive when we drive. If we become more aware of our own anger triggers, we will also better understand what provokes other drivers.

Driving While Black (DWB)

While there has been recent attention to DWB, or racial profiling of motor vehicle drivers, DWB is nothing new to many sisters. "It's something I've always been aware of. We grew up next to an affluent neighborhood, and it was understood that if you drove through that neighborhood, it was likely that an officer would tail your car and run your plates, so you'd better not have any outstanding tickets—but the real shame of it is that it still holds true today," recalls Shawn, a woman who is now in law enforcement.

Finally, racial disparities such as the one described by Shawn are being tracked in certain states, but the reality is that these patterns of stopping black motorists evolved out of the Jim Crow days and still hover today. Use the following precautions when you think you're being singled out:

1. Cooperate with the officer. What you consider intelligent questions can be viewed as belligerence by the officer.
2. Register a legitimate complaint with the police headquarters and your local NAACP chapter.
3. Consult with your lawyer for legal advice regarding your rights.

Fortunately, watchdog groups and state officials are addressing this issue. You can help yourself by watching how you respond if an officer stops you and you think it's a case of racial or gender profiling.

HOW YOU RESPOND TO TRIGGERS RELATES TO YOUR ANGER STYLE

African-American women's highest value lies in their interpersonal relationships. It is important for us to understand and value one another. When we experience problems in our relationships it can become extremely upsetting to us because of our value system. We need to examine our style of communicating when we are angry and recognize when we are exhibiting unhealthy anger styles. Research on over two hundred women for ten years showed that women with a behavioral style that holds in anger show physical signs that indicate heart attacks by their sixties. Women, more often than men, will cry when angry. Progression in the Invincible Black Woman syndrome indicates that a mild-mannered person with these tendencies may go off in a fit of unexpected rage. Our anger develops into stress-related symptoms from insomnia to cardiovascular disorders. Medical research gives us women reasons to control our anger. At an American Heart Association conference, cardiologists warned of the relationship between anger, heart attacks, and strokes.

The Authoritarian Anger Style

When angry, the authoritarian sister usually has difficulty seeing others' points of view or feelings. This person can be blunt and not realize that she is offending others by her harsh words. She argues in a direct manner and places herself and her abilities above everyone else.

This anger style is hurtful to others and places additional stress on the authoritarian because she often alienates others with this destructive behavior. For example, Karla, whom we discussed in Chapter 1, had an authoritarian anger style that she patterned after her mother. When Karla's actions did not meet the approval of her mother, Karla created anger triangles between herself, her mother, and her father, attempting to win the power struggle with her mother. Karla had difficulty seeing how hurt her mother would feel after arguing with her father about disciplining Karla.

The High Profile Anger Style

The high profile sister is concerned with her image and may put on a strong front when angry. Trying to make the best of a bad situation, she will attempt to remain optimistic and sociable. The high profile person especially becomes angry when she is not recognized or feels rejected. She needs to be aware of falling into the Invincible Black Woman syndrome of keeping up an exaggerated strong front and losing touch with her emotions.

The Pragmatic Anger Style

The pragmatic sister is a stable team player that is at risk of internalizing anger for fear of what others may think about her. This person enjoys a peaceful environment.

The pragmatic sister is also at risk of blindly going off after holding in her angry feelings for long periods of time. This person may fall into the Invincible Black Woman syndrome out of a need to please others and keep cohesiveness in a group.

The Intellectual Anger Style

The intellectual sister likes to be in control and feels angry when she is criticized. She wants everyone to adhere to set rules. The intellectual person has a difficult time understanding why rules are broken.

The intellectual person is sensitive to anyone criticizing her, but at the same time she is highly critical of herself and others. This person must become aware of negative self-talk that could lead her into the Invincible Black Woman syndrome where self-doubt turns into compulsive thoughts. She also needs to become aware of alienating the people she criticizes.

■   ■   ■

SISTERS WHO RECOGNIZE their anger styles can more effectively resolve conflicts between one another. Chapter 4 examines
the drama that arises in our relationships when we are not at
peace with our sisters.

Part Two

RELATIONSHIPS

4 WOMAN TO WOMAN

"I have never doubted that we were put on this
earth to help one another, to hold each other up."
—TERRIE WILLIAMS, *THE PERSONAL TOUCH*

WOMEN SHARE THE MOST intense and passionate relationships. From the wombs of our mothers into a world of male
domination, we practice a sisterhood that has survived a society
that undermines our self-confidence. Due to our second-class
status in society, we fight an internal battle as we struggle to maintain a healthy sense of self. Regrettably, we often engage in an
external conflict as well, attacking each other in our attempt to
advance. When sisters become absorbed in their rage, pain, wants,
and needs, relationships are often damaged and concerns for other
sisters fall to the wayside. Far too often, as a matter of self-
preservation in a culture where competition for black men is intense, sisters are taught not to trust each other. Some sisters
develop the "every woman for herself" attitude and injure others
in their quest to have a man.

All of our lives we are told about our weaknesses as women—
We are the weaker vessel. Is that why we feel compelled to put
on such a strong front? From the time we are in school, especially
junior high through high school, we receive less attention than
men in the classroom, especially in math and science. Through

academics and sports, boys gain greater self-esteem while girls in the same age group stop competing against boys and experience lower self-esteem. African-American girls confront gender and racial barriers, but they also deal with issues of appearance. How we cope with these challenges vastly affects our self-esteem as we mature.

THE COLOR TEST

Black women have often united through the organization and formation of groups. Consequently, our division within these groups partially keeps us disjointed. Certain sororities in the '40s and '50s would not allow a sister beyond the hue of a light brown paper bag into their organizations or their parties. The older generation of black folk remembers this clearly. If a sister with dark skin accompanied a sister with light skin, there were places that refused entry to the sister with dark skin if she failed the brown paper bag test.

Our current divide has less to do with skin tone and more to do with class. Some organizations set their barriers so high that a sister who doesn't have money for dues and activities can't afford to become a member. Even if she did, if she doesn't have a sponsor, she still can't get in. Some groups disappear because they make themselves extinct through exclusion.

As children, black girls quickly learn about differences in skin hue. We've listened to sisters who have experienced anger and pain on both sides: the sisters with light skin and the sisters with dark skin. The term "Black American Princess" referred to light-skinned sisters who had more privilege than their dark-skinned sisters. Black men with dark skin do not have the same challenges

SISTER CIRCLE NOTE #4

We share a history with our sisters that can never be forgotten. Let's continue to rise higher as black women and cultivate our relationships with our sisters through positive thoughts and deeds.

I will nurture my friendships with my sisters.

READ PROVERBS 18:24

within the race as black women with dark complexions. Dark skin on black men is considered masculine.

Before the '60s, when black was not considered beautiful, a black man with dark skin who wed a woman with light skin would brag if his daughters were born with a light complexion. Trina, a dark-skinned sister, married a brother with light skin from New Orleans. His family was "high yellow" and his mother and sisters treated her poorly. When Trina met his mother, she barely acknowledged her, gave her son a hard look, and retreated into her bedroom. This situation devastated Trina and, after facing obvious rejection, she grew angry and vowed never to go home with him again. When Trina had a daughter, she was born with a dark complexion and she did not have "good hair" like the rest of her husband's family. Trina argued with her husband about visiting his family because she did not want them to reject their daughter because of her skin color.

Myra, a sister with light skin, identifies herself as black but is often mistaken for white. She feels proud of her black heritage but vividly recalls the rejection that she felt as a child: "In junior high school, I was called half-breed names and girls picked fights with me. I wanted the girls to like me, so I began to buy friendships with snack and candy money that my mother gave me." Myra is comfortable now with her skin tone and when anyone wonders if she is "black enough" she doesn't care. Myra says, "Both of my parents are black and so am I."

Some sisters have a hard time identifying themselves as black. In our women and anger workshops, all of the women we surveyed were African American, but when we asked them to identify their race on paper, about 20 percent chose the category of "other." When we asked some sisters why they chose this category, they replied that they had white relatives or Indian blood in the family tree.

GOOD HAIR, BAD HAIR

Black women are the only women in America who face judgment about their natural hair and cultural style. This often creates situations of stress and anger when dealing with our tresses. When sisters attempt to wear their hair naturally, they are sometimes penalized if their hair doesn't resemble Caucasian hair.

Four sisters were going out to a club in the D.C. area and one of the sisters, Ebony, wore dreadlocks. She warned the other women that they might not be admitted to some of the trendy clubs in D.C. because of her hairstyle. The sisters looked one another over and decided that all of them looked nice and met the dress code. After all, these were African-American clubs that they were going to. When they arrived at the club, Ebony was held at the door. Ebony recalls, "The brother looked me up and down and asked me if I had a better skirt than the one I had on and then went further to talk about my shoes. I knew it was about my hair, so I left the entrance of the club before I went off. I'm thankful that my girlfriends weren't too upset with me because we had to leave."

Sheena wears weaves, braids, and wigs to keep up with the latest hip-hop look. She hates to go to the beauty supply store because she has to deal with the Korean shop owners. "I'm a loyal customer and everytime I go in there they watch me like a hawk, following me around every aisle. One day I just went off and told them that I was sick of them treating black women that way. They just looked at me like they couldn't understand English. The bad thing about it is that they own most of the hair stores in my community."

The trip to the store is only one of many annoyances that Sheena encounters. "Everytime I wear a weave or a wig, I have to hear what someone thinks about it," Sheena says. Sheena became angry when one of her friends told a man with whom she was developing a relationship that she was wearing a weave and that her hair wasn't any longer than the snap of her fingers. Sheena remembers angrily, "I decided to wear my hair short for a change, so I cut it and then I let it start to grow out again. My man friend looked at me with surprise because he couldn't believe how long my hair had grown. That's when he asked me why I had been wearing a weave." Sheena was shocked to hear that her girlfriend would offer up such information and indicate that she was nearly bald. Sheena wouldn't have cared if her romantic friend had discovered that she was wearing a weave naturally when he playfully ran his fingers through her hair. She usually laughs when this happens or tells men outright that she has a weave and to stop trying to feel for it. But she couldn't comprehend why her friend wanted to wound her by making a big deal out of it, suggesting that she was nearly bald. Sheena explained, "The next time I saw my girlfriend, I went off on her, telling her that she might get a man if she stopped chasing after mine. I could not believe my eyes because she was wearing reddish-brown curly weave braids. So I joked about her weave and told her that she looked like the lion on the *Wizard of Oz*. She developed an immediate attitude and our friendship became distant for a while."

Black women need to examine themselves in order to work on a collective consciousness of what having "good hair" really means. Dana, a cosmetologist, was concerned about her daughter Brianna's self-esteem, so she encouraged Brianna to feel good about her coarse hair. Brianna protested having her hair combed because it hurt to comb out the tangles. She was too young to have her hair permed and Dana wanted to protect her virgin hair. Dana always told her that even though it hurt, she had big and beautiful hair. One day during one of Brianna's protests about having her hair combed, Dana told her that she would have to have her hair combed like the rest of the girls at her school. Her daughter confidently commented, "They have flat hair; I have big hair." Although her daughter had painful experiences getting out the tangles, her mother referred to these tangles as love knots. Brianna was never raised to think that she had bad hair or told anything about nappy hair. Dana never conditioned her daughter to feel bad about her hair.

COMPETITION FOR MEN

Aisha, a college student, heard that a happy couple on campus better watch out because some of the sisters who were supposedly friends would thrive on the challenge of "taking" your man. At her college, sisters outnumbered the brothers two to one freshman year, three to one sophomore year, and by senior year the odds for a sister to have a long-lasting college relationship or prospect was slim unless she decided to date someone in the freshman or sophomore class. Campus life was relatively simple until she became involved in a serious relationship.

Before Aisha started dating Rahim, a campus football player with a muscular build and a rugged short dreadlock twist, she and her girlfriends always had something to say about Rahim, and he became a subject of common conversation among them. After a campus dance, Aisha hung out with Rahim and the two of them became an item. Aisha's girlfriends grew envious of her. When they saw Rahim riding around campus on his motorcycle they would flag him down at every available opportunity and feed him negative information about Aisha. Any girl talk was repeated. For example, Rahim began to question Aisha about an old boyfriend in her hometown.

Aisha began to feel that Rahim no longer trusted her and felt defensive even though she was faithful to him. When she turned to her girlfriends to discuss her concerns about Rahim, they would roll their eyes and utter a disconcerting sigh, signaling that they didn't want to hear what she had to say.

Rahim informed Aisha that he couldn't see her anymore because he didn't feel the same way about her as she did him. Aisha began counseling to have someone to talk to because she couldn't handle the rejection and betrayal she was feeling inside. She was devastated because within days of the breakup, she saw Rahim with her friend Gloria riding on the back of his motorcycle. Feeling that she was the source of ridicule, Aisha began to show signs of the Invincible Black Woman syndrome. She felt compelled to appear strong in front of her friends even though she had trouble disguising the hurt. Her image on the campus was most important. She held angry feelings toward Gloria for stepping into a relationship with Rahim so quickly after her breakup with him.

Aisha confronted Gloria face-to-face privately, and Gloria was non-apologetic, saying that she had her eye on Rahim first. Then Aisha went off on Gloria, called her names, and pushed her out of the way as she made her exit. At first, Aisha and Gloria weren't speaking to one another. Then Aisha noticed Rahim riding around campus with a new girlfriend. Aisha and Gloria got together and compared notes, and they realized that both were probably better off without him. The two girlfriends are working on overcoming the scars of the past and restoring their friendship.

Women well beyond the college years continue on a path that is not sisterly. Many sisters who have a goal of creating such drama in relationships, start out pretending to be your friend. They know your man, so they will be sweet and nice to you while they continue to inch closer to your boyfriend. When you question him about this woman, he'll accuse you of being paranoid and defend her sincerity. He may even suggest that you try to be friends with her.

Then one day the phone rings. It is the sista who was supposed to be your friend. She now wants to tell you what happened. Officially, the drama has begun. The type of person who does this hates herself, and when you dislike yourself, you lack compassion for your sister.

CORPORATE COMPETITION

A manager commented to a group in his training class that classes composed of males and females had successful levels of camaraderie. However, classes with all females were so competitive that they didn't make a good team. The sky can be the limit for a group of talented women that stick together to help ensure one another's success. However, sometimes when women are together in competitive situations, they regress to childhood acts similar to fighting over the last piece of candy. If women feel a scarcity of opportunities, they begin to push one another out of the way.

For sisters, the competition issue is more intense if we feel there is room at the top for only one black female. In some ways, our work situations are set up like a plantation. Some sisters call this the "plantation mentality," a situation where only one sister has close ties to the boss. This sister feeds any negative information to the boss that she gathers in the "field." Roshawn, an account executive for a telecommunications company, revealed her plantation experience: "I'm an executive and every time I went to our corporate office in Indianapolis, the black secretary would try to find out the scoop on what I was doing. If I came in the office with my hair looking fresh, she would ask me if I just had it done during working hours so that she could have something to run and tell the boss. Then she would try to have lunch with me to have more to report back to the boss. At first she had me fooled, but word got back to me not to trust her because she reported everything that I said to her boss. Just thinking about the fact that she had mentioned my personal information infuriated me. The next time I saw her privately, I went off on her for repeating my personal business to the boss."

Regardless of the level of our position, the corporate plantation mentality prevents sisters from leaning closer to one another. Lack of opportunity for upward mobility places us in a competitive position for favor from upper management. Often, when we have antagonistic relationships with one another, we will go off quicker than others in the office.

SUPPORTING A SISTA IN NEED

Is it our anger over unfair conditions that makes us so competitive with one another sometimes? Often women don't lend support to one another in the simplest forms. Gavin De Becker commented in his book, *Gift of Fear,* "I encourage women to ask other women for help when they need it, and it's likewise safer to accept an offer from a woman than from a man. (Unfortunately, women rarely make such offers to other women, and I wish more would.)"

In the women and anger survey, sisters discussed difficult times when there were no supportive sisters around to help them. The inability to ask for support from others led these sisters to fall into the IBW syndrome, suffering from stress-related conditions. There are troublesome times in sisters' lives when they need love and support. Sometimes sisters don't offer assistance to other sisters in need, and when a sister is in the IBW syndrome, she doesn't know how to accept help from another sister.

Cheryl, a twenty-five-year-old chef who lives in Cleveland, complained, "My friend Renée was feeling depressed and asked me to join her for a get-away weekend. I tried to be supportive to my girlfriend, Renée, but her boyfriend constantly interfered with our plans. I didn't like him and he couldn't stand me. When I called to pick her up for the get-away weekend she told me that her boyfriend said that she couldn't go. I had already paid for her plane ticket so I went off and told her that she was going." Cheryl was at Renée's condo waiting for her to pack her clothes when her boyfriend came over and went upstairs to talk to Renée. Cheryl was furious because she could tell by the way that he glared at her that he planned to prevent Renée from leaving. Renée came downstairs and quietly told Cheryl that although she wanted to go with her, her boyfriend said she couldn't leave, and she was developing a headache. Cheryl told her girlfriend that she was behaving stupidly, and that she had better reimburse her for the plane ticket.

Renée typifies a woman who is in the IBW syndrome because she has difficulty communicating her feelings and desires. In this case, she set aside her personal feelings to please her boyfriend. Women like Renée often experience symptoms such as headaches, a characteristic of the IBW syndrome, because they repress their true feelings, sacrificing their personal health and wellness.

MORE DRAMA FOR YOUR MAMA

Karla, whom we discussed earlier, always loved her mother but often had trouble communicating with her ever since she was a child. During Karla's teen years, expression of anger toward her mother was considered talking back. If Karla talked back to her mother, she could expect to see her mother go off, threatening to take her to juvenile detention, down south, or kick her out on the street.

Karla can't remember having any compassionate conversations with her mother about sexuality. As an adult, Karla reveals, "I was to the point where I couldn't confide anything to my mother if I had a problem with a man. I feared that if I told her I was feeling rejected by a man that she'd say, 'Why do you always pick those no good type of men?' Then I know the next comment would be the self-righteous story of her virginity until she met a good man, my father. And I know that I would go off because my father had affairs and a child outside of their marriage. So I would pretend that everything was well with my relationship. We were completely different personalities when we talked to each other—hiding our true feelings."

Karla's situation is not unusual. In order to avoid her anger toward her mother for not listening to her with empathy, she avoided confidential conversations. Many women share feelings about difficulty talking with their mothers. Somewhere along the way, women learn that talking to their mothers about sensitive matters isn't safe. Unfortunately, many mothers lose any chance to help their daughters cope with problems they face in life. In Karla's case, the admonishing that she received as a teenager from her mother led her to contain her anger. Karla laments, "Mom used to always tell me how bad I was and how I couldn't be trusted ever since I was fourteen years old."

Women who have experienced hurtful relationships with their mothers need to take time to understand them in order to forgive them. Harriet, a poet, remembers her mother working two jobs through the week and staying out late at night with her friends on the weekends. Harriet had everything that she wanted except the time she needed with her mother. That's when Harriet decided to make books a major part of her life and began writing poetry.

Harriet was accustomed to having an antagonistic relationship with her mother, but now that she is on her own, she has come to realize through counseling that her mother worked so hard because she was the sole provider. It was not until Harriet became an adult that she ever thought about the impact an absent father had on her mother. As a child, Harriet focused on herself and her own needs being met and she blamed her mother for not being there when she needed her emotionally.

We are witnesses of our mothers' quiet strengths. Our lives are different from our mothers in many ways, but in some ways things have not changed that dramatically. Although we have more opportunities than our mothers did, we generally maintain the same traditional roles in the household. Many of us are also single parents, and are therefore burdened with the additional stress that accompanies being the sole provider and caretaker for our children. Although some mothers did not have the perfect relationship with their daughters, they tried their best under the circumstances. We have a history of black women who have always worked, and, in the old days, took care of another family besides their own. At the same time, our mothers and grandmothers suffered abuses that are now inconceivable to most of us.

STEPMAMA DRAMA

Rhonda, twenty-four years of age, set herself up as a rival to her young stepmother, thirty-four years of age, who is younger than her eldest sister. Rhonda has lived with her father since her mother's death. She and her father had a close relationship, but since her father remarried, she has been angry and explosive. She feels hurt, threatened, and extremely resentful. She honestly believes that her father married her stepmother due to a case of temporary insanity and she can't understand why he chased after a younger woman. She's also concerned about her inheritance and no longer being the center of her father's attention.

Rhonda is not cordial to her stepmother and feels secretly jealous of her. She often goes off on tirades about "Dad and the witch." She resents anything that her father gives his wife. Rhonda called her sister, screaming and crying, after he bought his wife a diamond tennis bracelet. She thinks that her stepmother is a GDH: Gold-Digging Ho.

As a gesture to keep peace in their household, Rhonda's father bought her a new car. One day when Rhonda came home, her stepmother parked in front of the house where Rhonda usually parked her new car. She went into the house, going off on her stepmother about parking in her space. Rhonda's father voiced his displeasure regarding Rhonda's behavior and argued that his wife could park in front of the house. Rhonda couldn't believe that her father defended "the witch" and left the house screaming and crying again. Rhonda's eldest sister recommended that she begin counseling before it became impossible to communicate with her father. Rhonda is working on her issues, however she continues to express anger and harbor resentment toward her stepmother.

WE HAVE A rich history of sisterhood, one that tells us that it is possible for us to build intimate relationships when we trust ourselves. When we do this, we can grow individually and collectively. Trust in one another is one of the areas where we can begin to develop more support for one another. The outpouring of this type of sisterhood can evolve and heal us. When we honor our sisters, mothers, ancestors, and ourselves, we learn to use them as a resource to quell our anger and frustration as we face other challenges in our relationships and careers.

5 DEALING WITH MEN

"You tell a black woman you'll go off on her and
she'll tell you 'and I'll go off on you, too.' "

—BERNIE MACK, COMEDIAN

IN THE WOMEN AND anger survey, women from all
walks of life described the anger and disappointment they experienced in their search for the right men. The survey revealed that
women are angry because they have shared their feelings, fi-
nances, heart, body, and soul with men who later reject and/or
disrespect them.

Some people expect to see a black woman go off after she
hears a man make a provocative statement. Many black women grow tired of hearing about how angry black women are
and about ten to one odds, the saying "for every black man
there are ten black women." Most of the anger that black
women have in their relationships with men appears to serve
as a defense mechanism to avoid confronting their fear of rejection.

SEARCHING FOR MR. RIGHT,
FINDING MR. WRONG

Often we become preoccupied with our anger and disappointment. Since we are unable to release the past, we poison ourselves
in the present with obsessive thoughts about men. Our everyday
activities are consumed with how to keep the man we have, or
how to get a man we can keep. During a therapy session, Clara
spoke of her best friend Tina's compulsive attitude toward men.
Whenever Tina is expecting a man to call, she answers the phone
in a sexy, cheerful voice. If a woman is on the line, her voice falls
from obvious disappointment. "One day I called over there, and
she dropped her voice like that," Clara said. "I asked her who
she was expecting to call. Aren't I good enough?"

Compulsive behavior also creates a climate of what Noreen calls
"interference." Instead of allowing a relationship to evolve, we in-
trude. We play detective, or what some women call "getting to the
411," to learn the facts about the men we meet. Of course, such
snooping is not justified. It denigrates the man and belittles the relationship. It's as if we find relationships so terrifying that we must
arm ourselves with information. In such a situation, we do not experience a relationship with a new man. Instead, we continue our
relationship with our unhealed wounds, anger, and fear.

Fear masked with anger can take many forms. Sometimes we
avoid seeing what is really there by falling head-over-heels in
love. If we look closely, we can see that such an approach is
impractical and doomed to failure. When a woman does this, she
denies responsibility for the relationship through her projection
of a fantasy. Her reluctance to take time to get to know the man
before she labels him "Mr. Right" is another example of fear-

SISTER CIRCLE NOTE #5

Black women and men have shared a passionate love, one where husbands and wives who were separated during slavery searched for one another following emancipation.

I have room in my heart to have an adoring relationship that is based on friendship and love.

READ SONG OF SONGS 3:1–4

induced behavior. John, a first-year resident at a university hospital, described these dynamics from a male point of view. "I get tired of meeting women who find out I am in medical school and then decide I am the One. They don't even know me, but they decide I'm their future husband."

This compulsive behavior appears incomprehensible to outsiders, but to the women involved it seems appropriate and natural. During counseling, a court reporter named Terrie had this to say: "When I laid eyes on Zach, I thought I'd like to date him, so I gave him my phone number. I told all my friends that if they met up with a 6' 2", dark-skinned, well-muscled personal trainer to stay clear because he belongs to me!" Terrie's friends thought her behavior was odd. They felt she was setting herself up for disappointment and anger with a man she didn't know.

Loss of perspective often accompanies compulsive behavior. Women who obsess about their relationships generally are not able to drop the subject when they go to work and they share their dating experiences with their co-workers. Women want to talk about their lovers, have them visit the job site to meet for lunch, attend employee gatherings, and so forth. Men, on the other hand, are better able to separate work from their personal lives. If the relationship ends, women have to face their co-workers.

Katrina, a black woman in her twenties, was dating Tommy, a twenty-eight-year-old Native American man in Seattle, Washington. She decided to relocate to New York to work part-time while she attended nursing school. Tommy moved with Katrina and lived with her while she completed her education. After a while, Tommy began to meet Katrina at her office to take her to lunch. It was obvious to her co-workers that Katrina was smitten with Tommy. When he gave her an engagement ring after she graduated from nursing school, she showed it to her co-workers, and they were happy for her.

However, two weeks after Tommy gave Katrina the ring, he broke off the engagement. He told her that he could not marry her because his female cousin had a bad marriage to a black man, and he moved out of Katrina's apartment. The breakup occurred after one of Tommy's tribal celebrations, which Katrina was forbidden to attend because she was not Native American.

Katrina later discovered that Tommy's cousin influenced the breakup because she was looking for a man in the tribe; there was a shortage of them, so she wanted Tommy for herself. Katrina cried at work and was consoled by her co-workers, but it was an embarrassing and demoralizing breakup. She was furious about it and grew distracted at work, often forgetting details and slipping up on important matters in an alarming way. After the emotional scene, Katrina felt as if her co-workers must think less of her, and it was impossible to feel on equal footing with them after that.

This added to her feeling of inadequacy and low self-esteem. Katrina harbored self-defeating feelings for a long time, falling into the IBW syndrome. She refused therapy and concealed her problems with an artificial carefree attitude. She began to drink excessively and spend money on shopping binges, buying things she later didn't want or need.

Alisa, an artist with a bohemian flair, has gone off more than a few times in relationships. When she is attracted to a man, she often has intense emotions accompanied by erratic mood swings. She loves to be in love and becomes attached to the sensation of love. Afraid that she'll lose the sensation, she begins to cling to the relationship. The man she is involved with becomes resistant, which only causes her to cling more fiercely. Alisa panics and behaves crazily, often acting out her fear through bizarre expressions of anger. She behaves in immoral or inappropriate ways, eavesdropping, searching through her lover's things, spying on him, and grilling and questioning him about other women. Later, when she calms down, she feels guilty and embarrassed; her self-confidence plummets. Alisa described a breakup with a recent boyfriend: "It was late, and I kept calling James because I wanted to talk to him. He wouldn't answer the phone so I went over to his house. He didn't answer the door, but the kitchen window was open so I crawled in and went into his bedroom and woke him up. He really didn't like the fact that I broke in, and he wouldn't talk to me about our problem. There was another woman in the picture; he was planning to move in with her instead of me. I guess I felt really used. When I drove home from James's house at 4:00 A.M., I was crying hysterically. The roads were wet, and the light turned red, but I didn't care, so I ran it and hit a car. The next day, when I really couldn't deny anymore that the relationship was ending, I cut my hair because James loved it and that was my way to get back at him. My hair was down to the middle of my back, and I ended up looking like Grace Jones. I had put so much of myself into him. I gave up my art career temporarily and spent a lot of time and money on James. I wanted to hurt him because he really wasn't thinking about me."

Painful and nonproductive relationships create self-destructive situations that do not elevate our sense of self-worth and only increase our anger. We will discuss ways to deal with pain and fulfillment in relationships in Part III.

WHEN ANGER LEADS TO REVENGE

Tamara, a twenty-nine-year-old communications director, suspected that her fiancé was cheating on her and decided to begin her own method of being a player. Tamara suspected that women were calling her fiancé, Daryn, at his home. She began to search through Daryn's caller ID at his home and gather telephone numbers of women. She decided to call one of the numbers, but she hung up when the young woman answered the phone.

Although she was furious, Tamara didn't mention a word about the calls to Daryn. Holding in her feelings of suspicion, Tamara began to fall into the IBW syndrome. She didn't feel comfortable talking to her girlfriends about it because she needed to uphold her trophy as the first of her friends to become engaged, and she continued to portray the image of a happy bride-to-be.

Tamara's best friend broke through her silence when she mentioned to Tamara that she saw her fiancé at a restaurant with another woman on his arm. Humiliated and frustrated, Tamara went off and told her girlfriend that she was going to show Daryn that she could play the player. She had her girlfriend set up a double date at the same popular restaurant, and this time Daryn's friend saw Tamara with a date. Daryn informed Tamara that he knew that she had been out with some guys and he told her that he wanted to break the engagement. Crying and hysterical, Tamara angrily informed Daryn that he was seen at the same place with a woman and she slapped him in the face: "I purposely set up a scene with another man to make Daryn jealous. There was no love between us. I felt played and I wanted to show Daryn how it felt," Tamara says.

The playboy or playgirl mindset is a dangerous game when both parties set out to see who can score the most prospects. Tamara loved Daryn, but her method of trying to match player wits with him backfired. Physical violence was never in Tamara's makeup but her hand slapped Daryn's face while she was going off on him. Tamara had held so much inside throughout the relationship that she lost control when she and Daryn finally discussed the subject of cheating on each other. Through the breakup, both Tamara and Daryn were left with no love interest in the wings as each had led one another to believe.

Valerie had a rocky relationship with her boyfriend Leon. She loved the man but not his behavior. Early in their relationship, when Valerie attempted to socialize with her friends, Leon became possessive and jealous. He didn't want to share her with her friends so he began to take her out with him to clubs on weekends. Valerie knew as soon as Leon had a couple of drinks that he would begin to lust after other women in the club and accuse her of looking at other men. Leon would continue drinking and spending money buying rounds of drinks for friends that they could not afford.

Valerie didn't drink and really didn't care to go out with Leon but she remained silent because she wanted to please him. She was tired of feeling that she needed to go out with him to watch him. When Leon drank he would dance with other women. While Leon danced with other women, Valerie would dance with another man if asked. They would argue the entire ride home if either one of them danced with another person. Valerie wanted to show Leon that two could play his game but somehow those evenings always seemed to backfire and Valerie would internally blame herself. After two years of dating, Valerie felt that she was in a relationship that she could barely tolerate but she felt powerless about making a change in her relationship with Leon.

Mia became pregnant a couple of months before her twentieth birthday by her boyfriend Monte. Initially, they mutually decided that they were not ready for marriage and moved in together. When the baby arrived, they were living together in a cute suburban two-bedroom apartment—neat, but not too expensively furnished. Monte was driving a new red sports utility vehicle. They were able to live comfortably because Monte landed a job as a construction worker. Strong and young, he survived a tough environment and was soon making over fifteen dollars per hour.

Once the baby was born, Mia noticed that Monte seemed to grow more and more restless. When the baby woke up for her feedings or cried, Monte became irritable and withdrawn. Although he was never the type of guy to contribute around the home, the small things he did, such as take out the garbage, stopped altogether.

Mia tried to talk to Monte about his behavior, but nothing seemed to change. Or if he made an effort, he soon reverted back to his same old patterns. After several months of arguing, Monte began to avoid coming home and Mia suspected that he was visiting other women.

The first few times Monte was late, Mia fussed about it, but after some initial complaining she let the argument drop. Monte was pretty good about coming home on time for a while but, as usual, he began to repeat his previous behavior. The fourth time this happened, Mia was dressed and ready to go out looking for his car.

Though Monte expected her to be upset with him for being late, he wasn't prepared for what he did get—screaming, hollering, cursing, and threats from Mia that she would take the baby and leave him. In his defense, Monte stated that he needed some time out with the fellas and he felt as if she was smothering him. Mia decided that it was just fine for him to go out without her. The next time Monte went out she made arrangements for a sitter and went out with her girlfriends. But Mia was miserable. The player scene at the club was not her idea of a good time and she usually wanted to leave early. More concerned with drama, Mia tried to convince one of her girlfriends to drive her around to see if she could "catch Monte with another woman and go off."

Mia eventually caught Monte with a woman in his car and she went off on both of them. Mia was fighting Monte and calling his date names. Monte threatened to take Mia to court for assault and Mia threatened Monte with court-ordered child support. The situation continued with constant fighting and accusations until Monte decided he wanted out of the relationship. Since it was his apartment and car, Mia and the baby moved back home with her mother, and Mia was more miserable than ever.

Although Mia still thinks Monte was playing her, she feels that her handling of the relationship was definitely wrong. Mia asked Monte to change his player ways and allow her to move back in with him, however Monte told her that he realized that he was not ready for that type of commitment. Mia filed for court-ordered child support. Monte is assuming more responsibility with visitation and is spending time with the baby. Mia retired from her playgirl days and hopes that one day she will find a faithful man and get married.

SIGNS THAT HE IS ABOUT TO LEAVE

They say that love is blind. We have talked with many women who have had their eyes closed when their mates signaled that they were about to leave them. They see the signs, ignore them as long as they can, and then desperately seek help to deal with their feelings of betrayal.

The signals can be subtle or quite obvious. Of course, if your mate shows these signs it does not necessarily mean that he is leaving you. The signs are an indication that your mate may be unfaithful, or may be planning to end the relationship, but has not taken the steps to do so. The problem for many women is that we ignore these signs, falling into the IBW syndrome, making ourselves sick over the relationship. Or we go off.

If you familiarize yourself with these signals, it may help you to honestly evaluate the relationship. Seeing things clearly can keep you from going off or falling into the IBW syndrome. Bear in mind that some men use these subtle signs to try to break off the relationship gently and prevent a big blowup. Based on the women and anger survey, and the experiences of women and men who have been in counseling, here are ten possible signals that he plans to leave you:

1. NOTHING YOU DO IS RIGHT.
    What happened to the nice compliments that warmed your heart when you first met him? Now you're dumb, you

need a new hairstyle, you're too fat. Everything you say gets on his nerves. Don't snuggle next to him; it's uncomfortable. He doesn't like to hold hands. He doesn't want to eat the food you prepared. "I knew in my heart that he didn't love me anymore when he wouldn't let me cross my leg over his or play footsie with him anymore. It used to be the way we showed affection for each other," says Sandra, a retail buyer.

2. LOSS OF INTEREST IN SEXUAL PLEASURE.

When he changes lovemaking patterns from every other night to once per month, you wonder: Is he making love to someone else? Lillian, a computer specialist, revealed that she and her husband had not made love in six months. Following a joint therapy session, the couple made passionate love. After that evening however, Lillian's husband stopped making love to her again. She enjoyed it; he didn't. He said she didn't move enough; she was boring in bed, and so on. To Lillian's disappointment, the lovemaking she had enjoyed was simply a half-hearted attempt on his part to see if he could become sexually interested in her again. Eventually, Lillian did find that her husband was seeing another woman at work. Of course, changes in sexual appetite do not always indicate that a man wants out of a relationship, but if the man refuses to work with the situation, odds are he does have someone else on his mind.

3. HE'S CONSTANTLY OUT OF TOWN WITH FRIENDS OR ON BUSINESS.

You've known him to have control of his travel schedule. In the past, he would invite you to accompany him. His present busy schedule is telling you that he no longer has time for you, or that he may see other women on his trips. "When he came home, I unpacked his bag and saw packs of condoms," revealed Mel, an executive secretary.

4. **HIS PREVIOUSLY MESSY APARTMENT IS NOW CLEAN AND NEAT.**

He used to throw his clothes over the bed and leave his smelly sneakers in the living room. The floor always needed to be vacuumed. But now, his usually empty refrigerator has snacks and beverages; the carpet is clean. This change may mean he's got a new woman who he wants to impress.

5. **HE DOESN'T WANT TO INTRODUCE YOU TO HIS FRIENDS AND FAMILY, OR TALK ABOUT THE FUTURE.**

You may have big plans, but he doesn't. Don't force the issue if you recently met. Your fantasies may have let you down.

6. **HE TELLS YOU, "THIS RELATIONSHIP IS GETTING SCARY— YOU'RE TOO GOOD FOR ME."**

He has become emotionally unavailable. When he says this, often he's afraid to get involved, or he has lost interest and no longer wants to work on the relationship. Listen to the clues.

7. **NO MATTER WHAT YOU DO, HE'S UNHAPPY.**

He's unhappy about everything when he is with you, but he appears happy in the company of friends. You may be thinking that you need a change of pace, but he may be thinking about separation.

8. **HE'S NEVER HOME.**

You call him; he doesn't answer. He may be there, but he has caller ID, and doesn't answer when you call. When you finally catch up with him, he says that he's been busy. He may be trying to let you down gently.

9. HE HAS DRASTIC MOOD SWINGS.

He may be trying to drive you away with his mood. You thought he had a pleasant personality, but now you're seeing a different side of him. "He was interested in someone else, someone I knew, someone he worked with, so he was trying to push me away," says Mia, a realtor.

10. HE'S WORKING OUT AT THE GYM OR INCREASED HIS FITNESS ROUTINE.

He may be shopping around for another woman and wants to put his best appearance forward to make a good impression on his new dating prospects. Or he may be tightening up for the woman he's already selected. "I had never seen him work out so much, and he was always in the mirror checking out his muscles," says Cynthia, a beautician.

Sometimes when we are hurt, we cannot see how we hurt ourselves. Our own self-destructive behavior doesn't control a relationship. Instead it exacerbates a situation that is already difficult and increases the turmoil that we wish to alleviate.

6 RAISING CHILDREN

"I get tired of being everything—nurse, maid, lover,
psychiatrist, mother, sister—so I go off. And when
Mama goes off, the whole house gets quiet."

—KATHY

WOMEN OFTEN FEEL PULLED between career and
home in a way that men are not. Men can usually separate work
from home life, but generally women find it difficult because they
feel responsible for nurturing others at all times. For a mother
who is juggling career and family, failure to create balance for
herself can cause her to consistently go off on everybody in the
house or fall into the IBW syndrome. The need to have all the
luxuries of life also greatly contributes to this struggle.

BALANCING CAREERS AND CHILDREN

Mothers often feel guilty when their children let them know that
their absence from the family has an impact. They are caught in
the pinch between wanting to provide for their children with material things and having to work outside of the home to earn
money, and wanting to be present in their children's lives.

Tessa, a systems analyst, loved her job until she had her first child. She then began to resent her hectic schedule. When Tessa had her first child, she worked right until her delivery date. She was also the primary wage earner in the family. When Tessa returned to work eight weeks after her first child was born, she joined the ranks of other women in the office who always had to take extra time off to take the child to the doctor or leave early because her child was sick. Her responsibilities increased dramatically. She had to leave an hour earlier from home to drop off the baby at the day-care center and rush from work to pick her up from child care by 6:00 P.M. Her husband, Manny, worked for a shipping company and his delivery schedule didn't allow him to pick up the baby or drop her off, or help with doctor appointments. Tessa began to grow silently angry because she felt that Manny could have taken off work sometimes to help take some of the pressure off of her. Any time Tessa indirectly suggested that Manny help out with picking up the baby or with doctor's appointments he would give her a look that told her the answer was no.

Tessa didn't want to cause friction in the relationship so she put up a strong front. Trying to please Manny equaled internal frustration and stress for Tessa. Feeling like she was missing out on motherhood, Tessa grew jealous of the relationship that her baby was developing with their child care provider. Tessa's baby had become so comfortable with this other woman that when Tessa picked her up at the end of the day, the baby would cry. Tessa took out her anguish on the child care provider and began to accuse her of holding the baby too much. She began to feel guilty for leaving the baby with a sitter and not spending the quantity or quality of time with the child that she felt was needed.

SISTER CIRCLE NOTE #6

Humility and love can conquer chaos in family life. Share an idea with a family member today that may improve a relationship that appears dysfunctional.

I can strengthen spiritual ties in my family.

READ EPHESIANS 6:1–4

It became harder for Tessa to get up in the morning because she didn't want to face the day before her. When she left her baby at day care, Tessa would cry.

Tessa discussed quitting her job with Manny. However the discussion ended abruptly because Manny told her that she had to continue to work since she made the most money and they would have no way to pay the bills. Tessa became quick tempered with Manny and everything that he did started to irritate her. She would look at Manny and become agitated. Tessa was going off on Manny about frivolous matters and crying so much that she knew it was time to seek counseling.

Kathy is a good strong woman, an active member of Metropolitan Baptist Church. Kathy, a nurse, has three children and dedicates her life to working full-time, managing her household, and caring for her mother who has Alzheimer's. She hasn't had much time to participate as a member of the church choir because she spends her days working and evenings taking care of her kids and her mother. She cut back on her social life and is no longer a member of the Sisters Together social club. When her friends call and ask if they can help, she goes into the IBW syndrome phase of maintaining an invincible image and refuses their offers. Her husband works full-time and spends most of his spare time watching sports and sleeping. He's a member of Bedside Baptist— which means he doesn't attend church unless it's Easter or Christmas. Kathy lives close to her mother and checks on her every evening. She becomes frustrated with the kids when she comes home to find the house in a mess and has a tendency to go off.

DECLARING CHORE WARS

When Kathy comes home tired from the day and sees the house in a wreck, she explodes. She rants and raves, slamming pots and pans and threatening never to cook again. This is how she tries to attract her children's attention in order to receive some help with the housework. She always "goes there" when she needs her children, ages eight, ten, and twelve, to help with chores. Will, age twelve, was her greatest problem. When she would tell him to clean up, he would ask, "Why? Are we having company?" The kids knew that Kathy usually didn't go off about the housekeeping unless they were expecting guests. Kathy fusses the most at Will for not taking out the trash. It gets so piled up that they can't fit it all in the trash can for garbage collection. When that happens, the trash sits in plastic bags for another week, attracting cats and possums. The kids only help with housework when Kathy threatens to ground them or cut off video games and television.

Before Kathy can cook dinner she has to clean up. She can't understand why the kids don't willingly pitch in to help. When she asks them to help clean up, they tell her that they have to complete their homework or that they just returned home from soccer practice.

Kathy's husband becomes angry with her when Kathy yells and screams at the kids. When he says something to her about it, Kathy goes off on him, too. Kathy feels as if she's raising lazy, self-centered kids and she will go off despite what her husband says about it.

After she goes off the house grows quiet. The kids and her husband are silently angry with her. The children clean and grumble at the same time: "It's not my turn to do the dishes. . . . Mom gives us the hard work." Sometimes Kathy overhears the grumbling and places them on punishment for having a "smart mouth." They run to their father to intervene.

Kathy decided that she would seek counseling because she was tired of juggling roles and going off in order to convince the children to help her around the house. In her therapy sessions, Kathy revealed how hurt she felt because she did not have a united front with her husband regarding the housework. Kathy felt that her husband and children ganged up on her to make her look bad. She was afraid that her children might grow to dislike her when she only wanted them to do their chores.

TEENAGE CHORE WARS

Gloria is the mother of six children. Her eldest teenage daughter Erica is fathered by her first husband. Her other five children are the children of her current husband, Glenn. When she was interviewed for the women and anger survey, she broke into a rueful smile and said, "I had been cleaning house for two days in preparation for our two-week summer vacation—you see, I can't stand to return from vacation to find the house looking like a hurricane hit. While I was cleaning, I sent my seventeen-year-old, Erica, and fourteen-year-old daughter Trinity, to the laundromat. When I dropped them off I explained to them that I wanted them to fold all of the clothes. Erica's tone of voice agitated me, and where I come from you don't talk back to adults. When I picked up my kids a couple of hours later, I looked in the basket of clothes. Only the top ones had been folded. When I told the kids to stay and fold the clothes, Erica refused, so I slapped her in a fit of anger. She pushed me, and I took off my shoe and beat her with it. The manager of the laundromat called the police, and I spent the night in jail. At first I was so mad I could only think about how I was going to kill her when I got out. After I cooled off, I began to assess what went wrong and realized that it was about much more than some wrinkled clothes."

DEFIANT CHILDREN

Michelle, an engineer, sought family counseling to address the unruliness of her son Jason, age seven. Michelle told her therapist that she and her husband were "very educated" and they wanted a therapist with an advanced education—someone who could understand the needs of a child with attention deficit hyperactivity disorder (ADHD). In the family therapy sessions, Michelle often lost control and yelled at Jason. During one session, Jason began to kick Michelle and throw a tantrum because he wanted candy. Michelle screamed angrily at Jason in an explosive way that only resulted in more acting out by her son. After an initial therapy session, Michelle and Jason were referred to a physician specialist for a medical exam and medication evaluation. Michelle went off when her therapist mentioned that Jason might need medication. Michelle was concerned about what people would think about Jason and she refused to take him to see the specialist.

Michelle didn't deal with Jason's ADHD until she was called by his school. Jason had a tantrum at school and kicked his teacher. In the midst of Jason's acting out, he fell over a chair and sprained his ankle. Michelle was informed at the teacher conference that she was required to sign a behavioral contract before Jason could return to school. Part of the contract included a medical statement that needed to be completed by a physician. Michelle was angry about the contract and initially refused to sign it because she was trying to maintain an exaggerated public image and was concerned about what others would think. She thought about transferring Jason to another school but she didn't want a negative report to be sent to a new school.

Michelle signed the papers the following week and Jason had a medical exam and a medication evaluation. Jason was prescribed Dextroamphetamine. Michelle followed up with her therapist and began to work on dysfunctional family dynamics. Michelle stopped going off every time Jason misbehaved. Instead she practiced positive reinforcement and a method of discipline that fostered respect for others.

Within days of taking medication, Michelle noticed that Jason displayed more "normal" behavior and his teacher noted that he was more attentive in class. After a couple of weeks of practicing positive reinforcement with Jason, Michelle began to see remarkable improvements in Jason's behavior. It was also a revelation to Michelle that she had not been dealing with her own frustrations and that going off on Jason didn't help him develop positive behavior. Previously, when she had been unaware of the effect of her emotions, she had believed that she was always right and everyone else wrong. And she had felt that her anger that stemmed from maintaining a strong public image was justified. Now she began to see that she was often impatient and demanding.

When Michelle initially inquired about therapy, she was concerned about the level of intelligence of the therapist because her son had ADHD. However, in therapy, Michelle exhibited emotional immaturity or low "emotional intelligence," which has nothing to do with book smarts. If we want to improve our lives, we must use our energy and emotional intelligence in more productive ways than by going off. We must take care, however, that in our attempt to keep anger under control, we don't lapse into the IBW syndrome.

DEFIANT TEENS

When mothers begin to be challenged by their teens, they are forced to make difficult decisions on a daily basis. Examples of how these mothers of teens have been able to cope with these difficulties are discussed throughout this section.

Since her divorce, Marie's ex-husband has not participated in the parenting of their sixteen-year-old daughter, Nicole. When Nicole was taken to court by her school for unruly behavior, her father appeared in court to blame Marie for Nicole's announcement that she wanted to drop out of school. What made matters worse for Marie's parental authority was that Nicole's court-appointed lawyer and her father clicked immediately. Teaming up with Nicole's father, the lawyer stopped discussing the case with Marie or Nicole. Nicole and Marie sought psychotherapy. Nicole had been suspended from school seven times in six months for fighting. She didn't feel like she fit in with other students at the predominately white school because she was black, and the white male students taunted her. "I'm a young African-American female. It seems like the teachers hold it against me, too. They filed a charge against me at school for fighting a boy who called me a darky and tried to lift up my skirt. When he tried to touch me, he had gone too far; I fought him and won. I admit that I went ballistic and fought him like a wild animal. Sometimes I don't even know my strength or myself when I get that angry. I was suspended and taken to court, but no action was taken against him. When I tell the teachers what the white students have done to me, they ignore it. Because I knew I was in trouble after losing control, I voluntarily sought counseling before I went to court. I guess the most disappointing part of the situation, though, was having my father show up after practically no support for six years to tell the court what was wrong with me and try to prove that my mother was an unfit parent."

Marie was angry with the school principal for the way her daughter was treated at school, but she wanted desperately to help Nicole get to the root of her anger problems. When Marie visited the school principal to discuss Nicole's behavior, she was told that she would have to make an appointment in advance. Marie felt put off, but she made the appointment and met with the principal. Marie recalled the meeting: "The principal treated me in a condescending manner, and when I raised issues about how other students have treated my daughter, he ignored me. I went off on the principal and told him that because of the administration's lack of sensitivity, I understood why my daughter had problems at that school." Marie later regretted going off on the principal and feared reprisal from the principal regarding Nicole's reputation amongst the teachers. It was difficult for Marie to defend Nicole because Nicole fought any student who offended her.

After several therapy sessions, the source of some of Marie's anger started to surface. She had no support for her concerns regarding Nicole. Marie felt that, as a single black mom, she was treated with less respect than other parents. Marie remembered that one of Nicole's teachers asked whether her mother and father lived together. Marie was concerned about what the teachers and principal thought about her, but she decided not to dwell on it. She was struggling to do the best that she could for Nicole by living in a high-rent neighborhood that had a good school system, but it seemed that all of her plans since her divorce had backfired. At the court hearing she could hardly contain herself when she was viewed as nearly invisible by the court-appointed attorney after he met Nicole's father: "Her dad was so self-righteous in court, that he made himself look like a good guy and made me look like a villain." Marie had been in denial about her feelings since her divorce, and she wondered whether she'd ever find another man whom she could potentially marry. She decided to do something about some of her anger after the case was settled. She reviewed her divorce papers and filed paperwork for an increase in child support. Marie explained, "With an increase in child support I can do some of the things that he suggested for Nicole in court."

Margaret, the mother of Rose, a fifteen-year-old high school student, was angry with her daughter for getting in trouble at school. Rose and several of her school girlfriends skipped classes and went shopping. Rose drove them in her car and had the group at her house during part of class time. Rose was caught shoplifting, and she was suspended from school and viewed as the primary culprit. The school recommended that Margaret seek counseling for Rose. Margaret always had problems with Rose, her eldest child, because she had a habit of taking control of situations and going off if things didn't go her way. Following several sessions of counseling, Margaret made an emergency call for therapy. "You have to talk to Rose right now," she said, "She is out of control!" Since it was 11:00 P.M. the therapist asked Rose and Margaret to come in for therapy in the morning, but for now they needed to follow some ground rules for the rest of the night:

1. Rose was to do what was necessary for bed and call for a time out with her mother for the rest of the night.
2. Margaret was to follow the same rules, that is, time out for the rest of the night.
3. Rose and Margaret were to put the dispute on hold until they both could come in the following morning.

At the morning meeting, Rose had calmed down from the rage of the previous night. She explained why she had become furious and out of control with her mother. "Mom grounded me again," she said. "That was okay, but she ordered a pizza and wouldn't let me have any. I was hungry, and she wouldn't let me come out of my room to get any pizza; so I went berserk."

When asked her side of the story, Margaret said that she did believe heavy discipline and strict rules were the way to control Rose; however, she had not said that Rose could not eat. "I told her that she could come into the kitchen to eat pizza after she calmed down. And after she ate, she was to return to her room. When I told her this, she started screaming and swearing, and kicking at her bedroom walls. Margaret was furious and told Rose that if she didn't stop having a tantrum, she was going to call the police on her. Margaret was so angry that she thought about going into Rose's room and physically holding her down to prevent her from kicking the walls. Instead, she decided to call the therapist because she wanted to dissolve her anger before she reacted to Rose's tantrum. In her mind, Rose's anger was unprovoked, unreasonable, and dangerous, so she called for help. Calling the therapist helped Margaret to recognize the dynamics of the situation. Margaret knew that she needed to get control of Rose before they wound up in a physical struggle.

During a joint counseling session, Margaret learned that Rose did not tell her the truth about her sexual activity. Margaret believed that Rose was a virgin. Finally, Rose revealed to Margaret that she was sexually active and scared to death that she would become pregnant. Margaret asked Rose why she didn't previously tell her the truth and Rose replied that she couldn't tell Margaret the truth about her sexual activity because she feared that Margaret would go off and never let her out of the house. At first, Rose barely admitted that she experimented sexually, but later she confessed that she had difficulty saying no to any boy who told her that he liked her and that she was beginning to feel used by the boys. Margaret was angry with Rose for having sex indiscriminately and felt that she needed to change Rose's environment. Margaret sent Rose to live with her grandmother for a year to distance Rose's relationships with her girlfriends who conducted themselves in the same manner.

Helen, forty-three, experienced a lot of pain and anger when her youngest daughter, Penny, began to disappear during the evenings. Helen felt she had been too trusting with her daughter. When she tried repeatedly to talk to fifteen-year-old Penny about her whereabouts, Penny always brought up the issue of her older sister never being questioned. Penny repeatedly told Helen that she was picking on her because she was the youngest daughter and that she should be treated the same way as her sister. Helen responded by saying that Penny's older sister acted more responsibly than Penny.

When Helen asked Penny if she had a boyfriend, Penny acted squeamish and naïve, denying that she was interested in boys. One evening, Helen followed Penny and found her sitting in a car with a young man ten years older then her. Helen knew that Penny must have been sexually active. Out of frustration, Helen slapped Penny across the face before she knew her hand had left her side and threatened to prosecute her boyfriend. Helen knew she shouldn't have struck her daughter, of course, but she was so angry that she lost control. Helen felt that Penny was getting involved with a man that she thought was too old for her. After the incident in which she slapped Penny, Helen did not physically attack her daughter again. However, they did battle every time that Penny wanted to go out at night. Helen was less trusting and verified every place that Penny said she was going. Helen lashed out at Penny critically and harshly on a regular basis.

CHANGING FAMILY STRUCTURES

Erica and Gloria, mentioned earlier, were part of a blended family. Over the years, Erica had been the problem child of the family. Erica resembled her father both in appearance and mannerisms, much to Gloria's discomfort. When Gloria remarried, she encouraged Erica to accept her stepfather, Glen, as her dad, but Erica refused. Likewise, Glen never accepted Erica either. The dysfunction of the family had continued for years and was a constant source of pain and exhaustion for Gloria. Gloria was always angry because she was unable to dissolve the tension between Erica and Glen. Glen also had a way of insinuating that Gloria was too lenient with Erica. Gloria sometimes felt that she had to be harder on Erica to please Glen. Displacing the anger that she felt toward Glen, Gloria developed a style of shouting, hitting, and losing her temper with Erica. Erica thought she had the worst jobs in the house, and Gloria always told her that she was the oldest child and therefore would have to do the most housework. After the chore war incident over the laundry, Erica went to live with her biological father. Gloria feels that her household runs smoother without Erica, but she feels guilty, misses her, and is angry with Erica for calling her father and abruptly moving out.

Charmaine, a divorcée, is a single mom to seven-year-old Troy. Charmaine is financially secure but wishes that she could have made it work with her ex-husband, Ray. Charmaine boasts, "I'm really fortunate that I have a stable job and enough to provide a good lifestyle for Troy." Charmaine lives in an upper-class neighborhood and Troy attends a private school. Troy is involved in sports but Charmaine doesn't have time to attend his games and Ray is not a part of Troy's life. When they divorced, visitation was arranged through the court but never followed. At first, Charmaine was relieved that Ray didn't get in touch because she was still angry with him for draining their savings on a failed business and cheating on her throughout the marriage. Now she has heard that Ray has a good job and a new family. Charmaine is angry with him for not making any attempts to see Troy so she is planning to take Ray to court for visitation and child support. "It's not about the money entirely," Charmaine says. "It's about Ray never living up to his promises. He may have a new family but Troy needs his father, too."

Nineteen-year-old Shannon had her first child and moved back in with her mother. The apartment was too crowded and Shannon and her mother were always arguing about grocery bills and utility payments. Shannon moved out and enrolled in a welfare-to-work program. On the first day of the program, Shannon sat in on a "reality check" session that explained the job-training program policies. Shannon learned that she could not be tardy or absent from the job-training sessions. On Shannon's second day of her job-training program she was late because her government-funded child-care provider dropped her children off at school when they missed the bus and Shannon had to wait for her to return. Shannon knew that she was in trouble: "I walked into the training class and they told me that I had to leave and talk to a job counselor because they were considering kicking me out the program. I walked out and kept going. I called my baby's father and went off on him. I told him that I was taking him to court if he didn't start paying child support."

Shannon has internalized her anger and feels foolish for not listening to her mother's advice to get an education before becoming involved in a serious relationship. Shannon torments herself with thoughts like, "How could I have been so stupid to fall for him?" Every time Shannon talked with her baby's father she didn't know which side of her would come out: "It's like I was watching a split-screen video. On one screen there was the invincible Shannon that quietly convinced myself that I could make it without his help. The other screen was this time bomb waiting to go off on him for not paying enough child support or spending any time with the baby." Shannon doesn't know how she'll survive and is planning to move back in with her mother.

■   ■   ■

WOMEN NEED MORE support than ever when dealing with the realities of raising black children. When women constantly try to please their families and contribute economically to the family, they are at risk of lapsing into the IBW syndrome. They have guilt associated with working and leaving the home or they have guilt associated with not working or not making an economic contribution to the household. With a shift in government policies that mandate that all women with children must work, collectively women are under more pressure than ever to provide for their children and spend less time with them. Under the pressure of juggling different roles, women need to embrace one another while trying to maintain balance in their lives.

7

ANGER IN THE WORKPLACE

"I feel awful, like I'm disappearing, don't know who
I am anymore, for the first time in my life, I'm
losing myself, how can that happen? I'm all I
have . . ."

—JILL NELSON, *VOLUNTEER SLAVERY*

IN THE WOMEN AND anger survey, sisters confessed to having pleaser personalities, which caused them difficulties in the workplace. In interviews, sisters often spoke of encounters when they should have communicated with their peers or superiors and asserted themselves. Trying hard not to upset their co-workers or bosses, these women were afraid of the financial consequences of displaying improper anger in the workplace. They avoided confrontations with others even when it was not in their best interests to do so. Many of them continued to take on additional work assignments. Often, they increased the time and energy they gave even though they really wanted to reduce their workload and say no to new requests. In classic Invincible Black Woman style, these sisters gave more than they could be expected to give. They ignored their better judgment as they accepted more work. They were able to maintain an image of strength and reliability for a while, until something snapped.

SISTER CIRCLE NOTE #7

Many sisters' career paths take a series of twists and turns. Take time today to reassess and write down your career goals.

I can navigate my way around career obstacles through faith.

READ ISAIAH 45:2–3

FEELING SHORTCHANGED ON THE JOB

Some sisters keep up a strong front at work because they are concerned about what other people think of them. They allow others to take credit for their work, which leaves them feeling frustrated, angry, and disrespected. They may discuss these issues with a friend or co-worker, but they lack the confidence to speak directly with those who are involved. Asked if they had made any attempt at all to communicate with the person who had been the source of their discomfort, nearly all the women say no. A few say they had thought about approaching the offender but had been unable to do much more than mutter a few indirect remarks that went unnoticed. "No matter how badly I wanted to change the situation," said Jessica, computer programmer, "I couldn't even bring myself to take the first step, or to make the first constructive criticism. Usually, the best I could do would be to mutter something sarcastically or to say something indirectly. After that, I'd be madder than ever."

When Jessica was overlooked for a promotion that was given to a white male hired from outside the company, she was surprised and resentful. She had been performing the duties of the position as the department expanded, and her supervisor had praised her; there was no doubt in her mind about her ability to handle the job. "I couldn't believe it when they hired him from the outside. I had been doing the job for three months! And when they asked me to train Ryan, I was insulted. It seemed as if management thought I was qualified to take over and pitch in and even train the recruit, but not good enough for the job." Jessica began to wonder if management was giving her a not-so-subtle hint about her status in the company, so she decided not to rock the boat and protest training Ryan.

However, the training began to wear on Jessica, and she became lethargic, resentful, and depressed. Ryan, who was actually Jessica's supervisor, began to pass more and more of his work assignments on to Jessica. At a staff meeting, the boss gave accolades to Ryan for a project that Jessica had done. As the meeting continued, Jessica stewed. She was afraid to speak with Ryan about the matter because he was her supervisor, and she wanted him to like her. Ryan had repeatedly reassured her of how much he valued her contributions and how her good work would not go unacknowledged, yet at the meeting he was taking credit for the results while Jessica remained hidden in the background. Jessica spent many restless nights seething with anger and frustration over her job. Finally, she quit without having lined up further work. "I'd had enough," she explained. "It had gotten so bad I could hardly drag myself out of bed in the morning."

INSECURITY ON THE JOB

Sisters who experience the IBW syndrome at work become so preoccupied with maintaining their image of strength and reliability that they often ignore important things like happiness, health, and friendship. They procrastinate about making the decisions that might lead to improvements in their lives. Many times they see issues quite clearly and plan to take action. They are never able to do so, however, because they wait for the "perfect moment," which never arrives. Women suffering from the IBW syndrome see the world in dichotomies of "this" and "that," or "either" and "or" in the sense that they are unable to negotiate, compromise, or delegate. They feel that they must do everything perfectly, and only they can do all the things that must be done. They forget that life is filled with less-than-perfect people coping with less-than-perfect situations.

Because the IBW syndrome is such a rigid, inflexible condition, the women who suffer from it are often exceedingly hard on themselves. And because they are hard on themselves, they are hard on others as well. Such women seldom relax and are unable to relate to others in a forthright, wholesome way. Always concerned with keeping their guard up, they have a difficult time developing rapport with others. They dread communication, seeing it as always potentially confrontational, and they avoid conflict as much as possible. Consequently, these women put much of their world on hold. For instance, Jessica had rehearsed what she wanted to say to Ryan and the management staff, but she continued to wait "until the time was right."

Ironically, none of her co-workers could tell that there was anything wrong with Jessica. Her behavior gave no indication of the anger and frustration that lurked beneath her smiling exterior. Inwardly, she obsessed and fumed because she felt she was over-worked and underpaid. Outwardly, she set no limits and continued to allow others to take advantage of her capacity to work hard and efficiently.

The women who suffer from the IBW syndrome often feel insecure at work. These insecurities are related to basic fears of acceptance and rejection. If you experience emotions like these, stop and examine them. Are these insecurities telling you that you think you must receive approval from everyone? Are you maintaining your facade of strength in order to cover up feelings of insecurity? Do you tell yourself that you can accept things the way they are when the truth is that it really bothers you to do so? Are you developing symptoms such as tension, irritability, insomnia? Have you had at least one incident of an unexpected outburst of rage that left you with feelings of guilt?

Katy reacted strongly when she was excluded from a party given by the staff for interns. Only two administrators were not informed about the party: Katy and another black male administrator. Both of them felt they had been left out because the students they had chosen as interns were black students from low-income areas. When Katy walked to the office to ask why her interns had been left out of the party, she was told that Al, a subordinate, was in charge of the party. Upon hearing this in Al's presence, Katy banged her fist on the counter and yelled, "There is a racist situation in this building, and it must stop!"

Al wrote a letter to the Board of Education saying that Katy had behaved unprofessionally in front of students, visitors, and staff. Katy was later reprimanded by a senior administration official from the board of education for what was viewed as inappropriate comments for an administrator to make. "I had been angry with the principal and Al Brown since several of my interns had reported incidents that smelled of racism," Katy admitted. "The incident about the party was the last straw. My outburst was unprofessional. I should have dealt with the situation another way."

Katy's story illustrates the pressure cooker that Invincible Black Women can inhabit. Katy's emotional outburst made her look immature and extreme to her co-workers. It also demonstrated that the invincibility that Katy had taken such an effort to maintain through the years was only a veneer. Until the incident, Katy had been a well-respected, responsible administrator. It was difficult for Katy to inspire trust at work after going off as she did. Her co-workers began to pigeonhole her as "hard to work with" and "emotional." Katy's emotions did not interfere with her ability to do her work, but her co-workers began to treat her as if she were an emotional monster. And amid all this trouble, Katy still had not addressed what for her was the real issue, which was that she did not like her authority being undermined by those under her, such as Al. After being branded "emotional," she had lost so much credibility that her demands for authority were laughable, so Katy requested a transfer. Needless to say, Katy displayed an authoritarian anger style. Fortunately, she was hired at another school fairly promptly. Far too many women, however, become trapped in the workplace and ultimately face termination after outbursts such as Katy's.

WORKING WITH MEN

Mary worked as a dispatcher for the fire department before achieving her goal of becoming a firefighter. When she first started working as a dispatcher, she didn't announce her desire to become a firefighter. Working with men was fun in the dispatcher position because she admired the work of the firefighters, and always complimented them about the fine job that they were doing. She often received compliments from the firefighters about her work and how effectively she communicated information to them. Within months after she started working, she had been asked on several dates with different firefighters and enjoyed the attention that she was receiving.

Eventually, Mary did accept an invitation to go out on a date with one of the firefighters. There were no women working at the fire station and when she visited her boyfriend, Marcus, at the station, she felt as if all eyes were on her. Other men at the station would try to woo her from Marcus. Within a year, they were engaged. However, the engagement didn't last long. When Mary informed Marcus that she hoped to move up to the rank of firefighter, he was not supportive. Marcus told Mary that he did not want a woman that worked like a man. He also didn't think that she could pass the test or physical exam. They ended up arguing viciously over the matter and broke their engagement.

' Marcus proceeded to inform other men about her plans to take the firefighter exam. That's when things began to change. She had to withstand the brunt of many jokes. When she wasn't the subject of a distasteful joke, others would pry and ask questions. "When I first started working for the fire department as a dispatcher, I wasn't viewed as a threat. I was viewed as a nice lady, but things changed when I announced that I wanted to become a firefighter," she said. How Mary was able to achieve her goal and overcome adversity in the fire department is discussed in Chapter 10.

ANGER IN ACADEMIA

Since 1837, when the doors of Oberlin College opened to women for the first time, women have struggled to gain positions of power and status in academia. In fact, in the late 1800s advanced education was believed to be harmful to female physical and mental health. Eventually a report published by the American Association of University Women in 1885 debunked this myth. According to the U.S. Department of Education statistics, since 1965 there has been a steady increase in the number of women earning doctorates; however, there has not been a comparable increase in the number of women earning tenure. Universities are on the front lines of attack by opponents of Affirmative Action. These policies that have helped women successfully enter academic professions are at risk.

In the women and anger survey, sisters who have earned advanced degrees had plenty to say about their anger. Sisters have racial as well as gender issues in academia. Not only have these sisters expressed anger over their academic life, but they have expressed anger over the impact on their social lives as well. Black women in academia complained about the frustration of not receiving the level of respect that is automatically given to others. Many discussed having to prove themselves as tough or strong women to gain respect inside and outside the classroom. Choosing between a career and starting a family is also a major source of frustration for black women. Having children before receiving tenure could be detrimental to their career, yet sacrificing a family for job advancement could leave them feeling unfulfilled and lonely. Sisters with children are also less mobile than their childless peers, and they may find it difficult to relocate and retain their position. A brother, on the other hand, is considered more stable when he has a wife and children.

Virginia, twenty-six, shared the difficulties she had endured as a black graduate student in psychology. Virginia didn't feel as if she had a mentoring relationship with her adviser. When she would speak with him seriously about her ambitions and goals, he would laugh and tell her she was not realistic. "I cried when he told me I wasn't Ph.D. material. Then I grew angry and told him that he did not have a valid measurement of my abilities." Later, a male classmate who was a research assistant to her adviser told Virginia that she had made a big mistake. He told her that her adviser was upset with the way that she had spoken to him and that her success in the program was at risk. He told her that she better find a way to apologize. Feeling disillusioned about her major, Virginia went into the IBW syndrome and became extremely depressed. Determined to succeed despite the odds, Virginia then began to rely on classmates for help. "I had to lean on the guys in my class because they seemed to be the only ones who could get information out of professors about what I really needed to know to pass my classes. When the professor lectured, if you didn't know what the unwritten rules were, you would get ripped off."

Adrienne, twenty-eight, was thrilled when she was offered an administrative position in academia. "I felt that this was an important step between my master's and Ph.D. aspirations, and I planned to start my doctoral studies after my one year eligibility period for tuition benefits was complete." Adrienne's excitement about her position and further prospects in academia soon began to fade, however. Most of the ideas she presented to her director were turned down. Adrienne knew that her ideas were fresh and might work, so she took another approach. She began to feed her ideas through other staff members. It worked, but the staff to whom she fed ideas then took the credit and the accolades. That's when Adrienne began to fall into the IBW syndrome. "During my annual contract review I was told more or less that I was viewed as a young person who should feel lucky to have the annual contract renewed. I wanted to be seen as an important member of the team. I suffered silently." Adrienne began to develop nervous symptoms, and her hands trembled uncontrollably. "I was angry. Very angry. But I didn't want to get labeled as a troublemaker at the university because I knew any trouble could permanently affect my opportunities there." Adrienne was unknowingly staying in a destructive role, but she was determined to adhere to the role of the Invincible Woman even if it did affect her health. "It was becoming obvious. My hands shook, my eyes twitched, and people began to make comments about my weight loss."

After a year, when Adrienne tried to sign up for some classes, her supervisor refused to sign off on her tuition benefit papers because he told her that she would have to be available days, evenings, and weekends and that her classes would interfere with her work schedule. Constantly seething at work and wearing everyone's ear off at home, Adrienne knew that something had to change. When Adrienne's supervisor told her to come into the office after she had called in sick, Adrienne finally went off on him. Afterward, she says, "I knew that I had to explain my behavior, why I made those nasty comments, and when I did I was told that I was ungrateful." Finally Adrienne knew that in order to get well she needed a break from the stress of her current position. She resigned and obtained another position outside the university.

SEXUAL HARASSMENT

In the women and anger survey, many sisters reported anger about experiences with sexual harassment. Many had concerns about their job security and what others would think if they reported that they were being sexually harassed. Sisters who suffer silently while being subjected to sexual harassment can easily fall into the IBW syndrome. Remaining silent can also eventually lead to going off.

Since the 1980s, attention to sexual harassment in the workplace has intensified. Sexual harassment is defined as uninvited and unwelcome sexual attention. Despite the increased awareness of sexual harassment, it continues to persist, and according to national studies, women are more than three times as likely as men to experience some form of unwanted sexual attention.

Veronica, a computer programmer, experienced sexual harassment from a male co-worker shortly after she started a new job. As a new employee, she wanted to make friends with co-workers, but one co-worker, Don, pressured her for dates, gave her sexual looks, and gave her sexually explicit materials. Veronica said, "My stomach would churn when I heard his footsteps because I knew he was making his way to my desk. When I went to bed at night, I would close my eyes and see that piercing look he always gave me. I knew he made my other co-workers uncomfortable, even the males, so his behavior affected us all."

Although Veronica experienced discomfort and anger over Don's unwelcome sexual advances, she attempted to ignore his behavior to the best extent that she could. Exhibiting Invincible Woman tendencies, she did nothing about the harassment out of concern that others might view her as a troublemaker or weakling. She felt that as a new employee, the rejection of Don's sexual advances in an informal or formal manner might cause others to think unfavorably of her. One day she lashed out at Don and one of her female co-workers overheard. "You know, you don't have to put up with that," Robin told her. "Talk to Greg about it." Robin helped Veronica to put things in perspective, and she eventually went to her boss and discussed the problem as lightly as she could. To her surprise, Greg echoed Robin's words. "You know, you don't have to put up with that," he said. "I'll talk to Don." Don avoided her completely after that.

Felicia, a nurse, was in training for a new job. She received unwanted sexual attention from her trainer, Brandon. "Brandon harassed me with unwanted touching and sexual jokes that were blatantly stated in front of others. When one of the other trainers mentioned to me at lunch that he thought I was being harassed, I said it didn't bother me, although it did. I found it difficult to say anything, so the harassment continued. It felt like the longest training class ever, and I was glad to get through it. Brandon was never confronted or punished."

LIKE VERONICA AND Felicia, almost half of the sisters surveyed said that when they experienced sexual harassment they ignored the person and did nothing about the situation. Instead, they suffered inwardly, fell into the IBW syndrome, and wound up being less productive on the job. Many of them resigned or transferred from their position, choosing to leave the jobs instead of taking steps to correct the situation. Effective responses to sexual harassment will be discussed in Part III.

Part Three

SOLUTIONS:

A NEW PERSPECTIVE ON ANGER

"Anyone can become angry—that is easy. But, to be angry with the right person, to the right degree, at the right time, for the right purpose, and in the right way—this is not easy."

—ARISTOTLE, "NICOMACHEAN ETHICS"

8

DEFUSING ANGER
TRIGGERS

"Going off is a way that black women have to vent
the intensity of our feelings, but you must have a
plan so that afterward you know you definitely
affected some kind of positive change."

—TINA MCELROY ANSA

BEFORE WE LEARN HOW to express anger effectively, we need to learn how to identify our personal anger triggers in those experiences or emotions that can lead us to go off
or show anger in other unhealthy ways. Triggers are like buttons
connected to memories or associations that evoke anger within
us; each woman's triggers are unique.

TEN THINKING DISTORTIONS THAT
FEED TRIGGERS

When sisters have a negative internal dialogue, it affects how they
feel, think, and respond. The way we perceive situations often
stems from irrational beliefs or negative self-talk. For example,
when we view situations as "never" or "always" we are probably

overgeneralizing. When this occurs, we must ask ourselves what we are thinking or feeling and why. The following ten thinking distortions can help you understand and eradicate negative self-talk:

1. THE "TAKE NO PRISONERS" ATTITUDE.

    You have an all-or-nothing view and see things in black or white. This perfectionist attitude can lead you to fall into the IBW syndrome.

2. SNOWBALLING THE PROBLEM.

    You take a single negative event and your vision of reality becomes blocked; like building a snowball, the event overshadows everything, growing in size and meaning.

3. OVERGENERALIZING THE EVENT.

    Characteristic of the IBW syndrome, you view a single negative event as a continual pattern of loss and defeat.

4. DISCOUNTING THE POSITIVES.

    You overlook the positive experiences and find a reason not to include them. Negative beliefs are reinforced regardless of everyday positive experiences. This leaves you trapped in the IBW syndrome.

5. PERSONALIZATION OF THE PROBLEM.

    You attribute more value to others' opinions than you should. You also may view yourself as the cause of some problem. Women in the IBW syndrome often have these thoughts.

6. MAGNIFYING OR MINIMIZING THE EVENT.

    You exaggerate events such as your shortcomings or someone else's achievement, or you minimize things until they appear insignificant, such as positive qualities or someone's capabilities.

7. QUICK CONCLUSIONS WITHOUT THE FACTS.

You jump to conclusions although there are no convincing facts to support your conclusion.

8. BLAMING YOURSELF OR OTHERS.

You blame yourself or others with "should" and "shouldn't" statements. You're trying to motivate yourself with these statements but the emotional result is guilt. When you place "should" statements on others, you go off or fall into the IBW syndrome.

9. NAME-CALLING AND LABELING.

Like overgeneralization, you attach a mental banner across yourself that spells "I'm not good enough," when you make a mistake. If you are experiencing a negative reaction to a man's behavior, you may attach a negative label to him such as, "He's a scrub." You often go off when name-calling and labeling other people.

10. EMOTIONAL CONCLUSIONS.

You rely on gut reactions and negative emotions to reflect the reality of the situation; "I had an immediate gut re-action, so it has to be true."

HOW TO STOP TRIGGERS FROM MAKING YOU GO OFF

When someone transgresses a principle that we value, we often become angry or defensive. These ideals vary from individual to individual, but often contain expectations we have of being treated justly, or with equality, fairness, and respect.

The connection between triggers and going off is a sensitive one, capable of creating destruction. Frequently, women say things like,

"Don't let me go off," as if they can't control themselves. We must stop thinking this way and learn to take responsibility for our reactions. We have to learn how our personal machine works so that we can dismantle it. After we determine our triggers, we must remain aware of what is happening to us in the present moment. When we sense that we are in a situation that is likely to trigger going off, we need to develop the ability to defuse the trigger on the spot, with patience and resilience. When we fail and go off, it is a signal to seek answers from within and to learn more about ourselves and why we react the way we do.

RELATIONSHIPS

Anger in relationships is common among sisters. It's when anger escalates that sisters become stressed in relationships. When sisters go off in relationships, their anger lasts longer because of the intensity. When a sister wants her man to change and he does not follow through, it will trigger her anger. When this occurs, sisters need to identify the concerns that are specific to themselves and the situation.

EXPECTATIONS

Monique openly discusses her history of relationships with men. She seems to pick a new man for each year. Each January, Monique tells her friends that she is looking for a new love that she hopes will last. During therapy sessions, it became obvious that Monique felt angry when she encountered a particular type of

SISTER CIRCLE NOTE #8

As we move toward positive change in our lives, we will create conflict. However, we must not allow conflicts to destroy our plan.

I will manage my anger and not allow anger to manage me!

READ 2 TIMOTHY 2:23–24

personality she called the "Cheap Man." One involvement with a Cheap Man named Don lasted from February through December. When December came, Don completely ignored both Monique's birthday and Christmas. After the holidays, Monique broke up with Don.

Monique met Carl early the next year and began a relationship with him. When her birthday again approached, Monique began to anticipate that she might receive a friendship or engagement ring from Carl. To Monique's disappointment, Carl sent her a birthday card in the mail and came over for the usual pizza and romance on Friday night. "When I saw him come in with that bag that he kept his prophylactics in, and no birthday present for me, I could have screamed," Monique said angrily. "But I kept my composure and showed him his way to the door in ten minutes." Although Christmas was only one week away, Monique didn't hear from Carl during the holidays. In fact, he never called her again. Given her many experiences with Cheap Men, Monique grew especially sensitive about how her boyfriends treated her during the holidays.

After the breakup with Carl, Monique vowed that she would never feel used for sex again. To avoid the nervous misery of anticipating whether she would receive the gifts she wanted, Monique would become more critical of her dates as the holidays approached and would usually end the relationship. She felt relief not to have to compare notes with her friends about what her boyfriend gave her for her birthday or Christmas. Through therapy, Monique came to realize that she felt that if a boyfriend gave her gifts it meant that he respected and desired her. Without this form of approval, Monique would find it difficult, if not impossible, to maintain a relationship. She was also, she learned, susceptible to strong displays of anger and frustration during the holidays because she had emotional triggers from childhood wired to these events. When Monique was a child, sometimes she didn't receive the gifts that she wanted for Christmas or birthdays. Monique was often upset with her parents when she didn't receive a requested toy. As she grew up, she projected similar expectations onto her boyfriends.

Sisters should feel treasured during the course of their relationship with a man, not only on holidays or birthdays. Consider the following suggestions to avoid breakups over gifts:

1. AVOID FANTASIZING OVER GIFTS.

   If your relationship is not at a serious level of commitment, don't expect an item like fancy, expensive jewelry. Expensive jewelry does not make a relationship something that it is not.

2. DISCUSS INTENTIONS.

   Decrease gift anxiety by deciding to mutually exchange gifts and set an approximate amount that you will spend. Agree to obtain gift receipts.

3. ASK FOR GIFT-GIVING HINTS.

    Ask the person whom you're selecting a gift for to give you several suggestions or go window-shopping to discreetly identify their tastes.

4. STICK TO YOUR BUDGET.

    If your budget is small, stick to the set amount. Expectations that a sacrificial gift will provide an unfulfilled spark in a relationship may create great disappointment.

5. DON'T FOCUS ON COMPETITIVE COMPARISONS.

    When you discuss gifts that you received with relatives or friends, don't become fretful by comparing gifts.

HOLIDAY PRESSURE

At age thirty-six, after years of choosing to be single, Sibyl began to look for a man to settle down with. Her customary method of meeting men had been to frequent bars with her female co-workers. She was out at her Friday night hangout with her two best friends when she decided to move on to another nightclub where she thought she might have better prospects of finding a date. The following Monday, Sibyl bragged to her friends that she had been absolutely correct—she met William and he was a keeper. She reasoned that she was falling head-over-heels in love and they might elope in thirty days. New Year's Eve was only two weeks away, and Sibyl made elaborate plans for what she thought might be the best New Year's Eve ever, remembering how pitiful she was when she brought in the last two New Years alone with her television. Despite Sibyl's hopes and plans, William stood her up on New Year's Eve. Sibyl was furious and vowed to never "set herself up" like that again. Every time she thinks about

William, Sibyl thinks she'll spend the next New Year alone rather than face the prospect of being stood up again.

Of course, holidays or special occasions always evoke a variety of different emotions, but we should become especially aware of those events that stir feelings of anger. For example, weddings are often a trigger for those who have been hurt by the breakup of a serious relationship, or who are searching for a companion.

Amber, a divorced instructor at a community college, received an invitation to the wedding of her colleague, Rochelle. While Rochelle was engaged, Amber constantly dispensed advice about how to marry a man. When Rochelle married, Amber did not attend the wedding. Rochelle later called Amber to ask her why and Amber's response was "Did you think that I actually wanted to see you in a wedding dress walking down that aisle?"

Although Amber never discussed her ex-husband, the pain of their divorce was still present. For seven years, Amber had masked her feelings by assuming the role of the Invincible Woman. Amber advised everyone on how to keep a man, when actually she herself needed advice and support. Amber projected onto others the pain she felt about her own failed marriage. Weddings triggered Amber's bitterness from the past and the hopelessness she felt about her future prospects of marriage.

RACIAL TRIGGERS

Cindy, a twenty-year-old, was especially sensitive about her skin color. One day she was at the snack bar of a department store waiting her turn to be served when several white people stepped up behind her. The waitress, who was also white, came to the counter and said, "Who's next?" Cindy felt angry because she

WRITE DOWN YOUR TRIGGERS ABOUT HOLIDAYS AND SPECIAL EVENTS.

What do you say to yourself about these events that upsets you?

YOUR BIRTHDAY

_____

_____

_____

_____

_____

CHRISTMAS OR KWANZAA

_____

_____

_____

_____

_____

VALENTINE'S DAY

_____

_____

_____

_____

_____

NEW YEAR'S EVE

_____

_____

_____

_____

_____

WEDDINGS

_____

_____

_____

_____

_____

PREGNANCIES

_____

_____

_____

_____

_____

DEATHS/FUNERALS

_____

_____

_____

_____

_____

DIVORCES

_____

_____

_____

_____

_____

OTHER SIGNIFICANT OCCASIONS

_____

_____

_____

_____

_____

thought the waitress had seen her standing there and knew she was in line next to be waited on. "My blood was boiling and I was getting ready to let the waitress have a piece of my mind," Cindy said. "Then I realized that this was the way the waitress treated all the customers, white or black. Apparently, she didn't pay any attention to what was going on, so she had to continue asking, 'Who's next?' I took it personally because many times in the past white people have snubbed me."

China, a divorced thirty-year-old accountant, talked with a white male colleague about dining at a popular restaurant. He informed China that a friend of his worked at the restaurant and said that the white wait staff provided terrible service to blacks "because blacks do not tip." When China heard this, she was tempted to go to the restaurant and go off if a waiter even looked at her the wrong way. However, she felt it would be better to break any stereotypes that the waiters had about black customers. To test this, China made reservations and dined at the restaurant, leaving a twenty-five percent tip on the table. She then asked the waiter to return because she had decided to order dessert. When the waiter saw the tip, China received excellent service. In fact, the waiter trotted over to her when China asked for her final check.

GENDER AND RACE

Beth and Dominique, retail buyers, related an incident they had experienced in a restaurant that had a thirty-minute wait for seating. Since there was no wait to sit in the lounge, Beth and Dominique sat down there to receive faster service. While they were waiting, several white businessmen arrived and sat at the nearby table. Much to Dominique and Beth's surprise and irritation, the men were immediately given menus and their orders were taken. During the twenty minutes that passed, the waiter ignored Domnique and Beth. After several unsuccessful attempts of hand signaling to the waiter, Domnique walked to the bar and picked up two menus. The women were both beginning to become rather angry when the server started to bring out food for the men. When Dominique finally caught the eye of the server, he motioned for her to wait while he took orders from two black men who had seated themselves. Beth and Dominique were served next, and the waiter became more attentive as the restaurant crowd diminished. Before they paid for their meal, the server apologized to Beth and Dominique, explaining that the restaurant staff was not prepared for the lunch rush. The women exchanged kind words with the server, and the anger and frustration they previously felt changed to smiles.

Several times during Beth and Dominique's lunch, their anger was triggered. They found it aggravating to watch others served ahead of them and they had begun to feel that males of either race were given priority. Actually, the selection of the lounge seating was a poor choice because the wait was longer there than the thirty-minute wait in the main dining area. The lounge crowd was composed of a mix of patrons who seated themselves to drink, eat, or do both. Their server had more tables to wait on than did servers in the main dining area of the restaurant.

Ask yourself the following questions to help you control your anger when you are out in public:

1. **What unflattering feelings and behaviors will I show if I allow someone to trigger my anger?**

   "I will become angry and upset and go off."

2. What is unreasonable or inappropriate about my thinking in such situations?

"I take the treatment personally and assume that I am being singled out because I am black and a woman. Why do I assume that I know what she is thinking or feeling, or what her intentions are? Why am I so touchy and so quick to jump to conclusions? What is the chip on my shoulder? Why are my perceptions influenced by my emotions, and why are my emotions so influenced by my perceptions? Am I projecting?"

3. How can I challenge my thinking?

"The server is busy; maybe she really doesn't know who is next. Must I make myself go off because she did not see me standing here first?"

4. What reasonable options can I substitute for my unreasonable thinking?

"I appreciate fast service, and the help here is so slow. This is not the worst situation possible, but it is frustrating. My gender or skin color may or may not be a factor, but in any case I have the option of speaking with a manager. I could also relax and have a good time even though things are not going the way I like them to go. Even if the server is prejudiced against blacks, I don't have to let her behavior affect my attitude. I can do something about my reactions and enjoy myself no matter how unpleasant things become."

DEALING WITH CHANGE

Change triggers the fears that you have within. These triggers are magnified by the amount of stress and disequilibrium you experience in a short span of time. How you respond to change determines whether you will lose control and go off, remain in denial and fall into the IBW syndrome, or move forward with a positive attitude.

Taylor, a customer service representative, felt that things were going smoothly in her relationship until she discovered her fiancé, Chris, was seeing other women whom he described as "friends." Taylor was angry and hurt, but she felt like she needed to show Chris that she was strong. Without prior discussion, she postponed the wedding date, hoping that Chris would object, but he didn't. Frustrated by his acceptance of postponing the wedding, Taylor decided to make herself unavailable to Chris by overcommitting herself and not answering her telephone. Taylor became consumed with negative thoughts about Chris. However, Taylor would ask Chris to accompany her for occasions when she needed a date to maintain her image of a bride-to-be. When Chris visited Taylor she would make negative comments, yet deny that anything was wrong. When Chris was ready to leave, she would cry, and demand that he make love to her.

Finally, Taylor and Chris sought premarital counseling. Through counseling, Chris relayed to Taylor that he loved her and wanted to spend the rest of his life with her, and they both agreed to demonstrate their commitment by terminating casual friendships with the opposite sex. When she discovered that he had female friends, Taylor admitted that she was afraid that Chris might cheat on her. Taylor had fallen into the IBW syndrome.

When she needed to express her feelings appropriately to Chris, she decided to withdraw from him and fill her life with more chaos than ever. Women who exhibit IBW syndrome tendencies during a change deal with their triggers and fears by going into denial, overcompensating and overcommitting.

Consider the following ten suggestions for dealing with change:

1. DON'T ISOLATE YOURSELF.
   Spend time with others who foster a sense of consolation and care.

2. WRITE YOUR FEARS DOWN ON PAPER.
   Ask yourself, what is most threatening about this change in my life?

3. AVOID NEGATIVE SELF-TALK.
   Negative self-talk leads to a pessimistic view about change.

4. AVOID SELF-BLAME.
   Self-blame places us in the victim's seat of change.

5. APPROACH LIFE WITH A PURPOSE.
   Plan each day and include good nutrition and exercise.

6. SEEK COUNSELING.
   Therapy is a place where you can discuss your feelings and thoughts in a nonjudgmental environment.

7. HAVE PATIENCE AND UNDERSTANDING.
   Stay focused in your thinking and leave room for flexibility.

8. LOOK FOR OPPORTUNITIES.
   Develop a challenging attitude regarding change.

9. SET LIMITS.
   Avoid additional anxiety-provoking responsibilities during the change process.

10. **ANTICIPATE FUTURE CHANGES.**

Take a proactive approach toward change by validating your self-worth and the ability to manage your situations.

Sometimes we go into denial when betrayed by others until we face the reality of the situation. Behind the denial, we see the anger toward the person who has committed the offense. Sometimes we feel victimized with despair before we accept the situation. In order to resolve issues of betrayal, consider the following:

1. Honestly examine your circumstances.
2. Remember the good times without anger, guilt, or remorse.
3. Adjust to new frontiers in life, without fear that someone will betray you.
4. Acknowledge your feelings; it's okay to feel sadness from time to time.
5. Make room in your heart for forgiveness in areas where you feel that people betrayed you based on a lack of knowledge and understanding.

RESPONDING TO ROAD RAGE

In Chapter 3, we discussed road rage as an anger trigger. There are two types of road rage: women who fall into road rage themselves; and women who are victims of road rage, or who are reacting to the road rage of others. Males are generally the worst offenders, so we must be alert that we do not become the targets of their rage. As mentioned earlier, responding to hostility by going off can put us in an extremely dangerous situation.

HANDLING BETRAYAL

If someone deserts you in a time of need, or commits a treacherous offense, it takes hard work to mend the relationship and rebuild trust. Part of how you respond is related to how you've dealt with difficult situations in the past. First, answer the two following questions regarding how you've handled betrayal.

1. WHAT TYPE OF BETRAYAL HAVE YOU EXPERIENCED THAT YOU HAVE HAD DIFFICULTY ADJUSTING TO?

_____

_____

_____

_____

_____

2. WHAT PROBLEMS HAVE BLOCKED THIS ADJUSTMENT?

_____

_____

_____

_____

_____

We can do little to change a driver who has surrendered to road rage, but we can change how we react to the provocation. If you find yourself in a vulnerable situation on the road, or to avoid problems, try the following:

1. Avoid running late. Give yourself plenty of time to reach your destination.
2. Become aware of triggers for road rage in communities where new traffic has outpaced the building of roads.
3. Avoid exchanging obscene gestures.
4. Drive following the Golden Rule. Let someone in a lane or off a ramp. People generally respond to kindness with kindness. Texans refer to this as "drive friendly."
5. Avoid eye contact with an offender; instead, record the license plate number and notify police.

RESPONDING TO SEXUAL HARASSMENT

The behaviors that are being defined as sexual harassment are broadening. Women, especially under the age of thirty-five, are at greater risk of being targets of unwanted sexual attention. Men are sometimes oblivious of the impact their behavior has on women. However, accepting this behavior is one of the least effective things we can do as women; it can lead us into the IBW syndrome.

The following three actions can help you eliminate harassing behaviors:

1. ASK OR ASSERTIVELY TELL THE PERSON(S) TO STOP.
   Women can improve the situation by confronting harassers. Elaine, a twenty-two-year-old women and anger respondent ex-

plained: "During the first three months that I worked at the company where I am presently employed, my supervisor interrupted my work daily to harass me with invitations. When I finally told him that I had absolutely no romantic interest in him he stopped. To my astonishment, he had no idea how much stress this caused me or that his actions were inappropriate."

Ann, a twenty-eight-year-old secretary, who changed jobs twice in order to avoid harassment, finally began to speak up for herself when her new boss began "flattering" her with his attentions. "I made it obvious that he was out of line by responding in a loud voice, 'What did you say?' When I told him directly that I thought his behavior was inappropriate, he stopped bothering me. It felt good to assert myself instead of changing jobs."

2. REPORT THE BEHAVIOR TO A SUPERVISOR OR OFFICIAL.

It can be more helpful to report a problem to a supervisor than to not report it. Becky, a thirty-year-old word processor was surprised by her experience. "I decided not to go to my supervisor at first because I didn't want to bother him. I was new on the job, and I didn't want him to think that I was disrupting the office in any way. After two weeks of being pursued and teased in an almost adolescent way by one of my co-workers, I went to my supervisor. I really didn't like reporting this activity because I'm very independent, and I like to think that I can handle situations personally; but going to my supervisor turned out to be the right thing to do. He immediately corrected the situation as soon as I made him aware of it."

3. FILE A GRIEVANCE OR COMPLAINT.

While most women do not file an official complaint, it is a legal option to stop the harasser and requires an investigation. Although effective in eliminating the harassment, some women have experienced adverse effects in the employment arena afterward.

CHECK YOUR ANGER STYLE BEFORE RESPONDING TO TRIGGERS

If you know your anger style, you can also predict how you may respond to a particular situation when your anger is triggered. Different styles require different methods of tackling triggers. Using your internal dialogue, you can prevent triggers from going off easier by knowing your style and how you might respond if you did not conscientiously think about how you were responding. At the same time, by recognizing your style, you can also prevent yourself from exhibiting IBW syndrome tendencies by internalizing anger.

The Authoritarian Response

When an authoritarian sister is responding to a trigger, she often blurts out exactly what she is thinking without considering the feelings of the other person or the consequences of her actions. Her internal dialogue often takes on the "take-no-prisoners attitude" where she only sees the situation from her point of view. She will meet resistance from others with this type of attitude. What this sister must think about before responding is: "Am I thinking from a one-way perspective? Am I jumping to conclusions? Do I want to destroy this relationship by saying hurtful things? Do I need to cool down before I respond?"

The High Profile Response

The high profile sister tries to tell herself that she is not angry by putting up a strong front. This sister often reveals that she is upset through her body language although she is not verbalizing her anger. The high profile sister needs to think about the following before she responds to triggers: "Do I feel rejected? Am I upset because I'm not the center of attention? Am I feeling like someone has one up on me? Am I upset over someone else's success?"

The Pragmatic Response

Seeking approval from others, the pragmatic sister often avoids conflicts. She deals with friction by holding in her anger. Occasionally, the pragmatic sister will lose control and go off when faced with opposition. When this happens, she often has regrets about the incident, because she views herself as the glue that holds her relationships together. When anger is triggered, the pragmatic sister needs to check her internal dialogue: "Am I giving more weight to others' opinions than I should? Am I allowing my negative emotions to draw conclusions regarding this situation? Am I avoiding confrontation?"

The Intellectual Response

The intellectual sister is concerned about being in control. Her anger triggers are more likely related to feeling that someone has stepped beyond his or her boundaries. She responds by correcting others with criticisms. When anger is triggered, the intellectual sister needs to consider the following: "Am I reacting to criticism? Am I blaming others or myself? Am I exaggerating others' shortcomings?"

■　　■　　■

EVERYONE HAS TRIGGERS. Figuring out what our personal triggers are and our anger style can give us the confidence to resolve conflicts with patience. Give yourself a chance to respond to a trigger by placing some distance between yourself and the person that has provoked you. This will give you some time to think about what you're reacting to, and it will enable you to calm down and think about the situation rationally.

Going off or expressing anger triggers is an outward display of anger. Often, sisters don't think through situations before going off or becoming provoked by triggers. Women in the IBW syndrome disguise their anger in an attempt to show strength. Intensely going off or overcompensating to hide anger are unhealthy ways to cope with problems. Chapter 9 identifies ways to break out of the IBW syndrome.

9 RENEWAL FROM THE INVINCIBLE BLACK WOMAN SYNDROME

> "You gain strength, courage, and confidence by
> every experience in which you stop to look fear in
> the face."
>
> —ELEANOR ROOSEVELT

MANY TIMES WHEN WOMEN recount their personal histories, we are struck by their level of denial. When questioned about their pain, they often fall into Invincible Black Woman routines, either denying the discomfort they have so graphically described or minimizing its effects by arguing that they have received strength or courage from their pain. In short, they appear to be out of touch with their feelings.

Women in the IBW syndrome are unrealistic about the demands they make upon themselves. They tend to be perfectionists and workaholics. These women must learn to slow down, to assess situations realistically, and to remind themselves, "It's okay if I'm not perfect." Women who manage both households and careers tend to measure themselves against incredible standards. They need to break apart or "unlearn" their old habits of expecting too much of themselves. They should examine their patterns, asking

SISTER CIRCLE NOTE #9

African-American women who suffer from over-whelming stress can find strength by facing their fears and leaning on a higher power.

I will feed my spirit with an active belief in the renewal of my faith through God.

READ ISAIAH 40:31

questions such as, "Why am I doing this? Why do I think I should do this? Who benefits from this? What will the result be?" The process of answering these questions can eliminate the mechanical responses and provide clarity, challenging women to examine the inefficiency of their perfectionist habits. A more realistic view of the world will emerge, and the Invincible Black Woman should find herself more in touch with her feelings. Asking these questions can alleviate stress and help her to feel happier.

IDENTIFYING THE INVINCIBLE BLACK WOMAN SYNDROME

Identifying the IBW syndrome includes an examination of your emotional health as well as your physical condition. Health signals are important because chronically holding in anger leads to many physical symptoms and illnesses. The discussion on negative self-talk will help identify a negative self-fulfilling prophecy. Perfectionistic tendencies can lead to unrealistic expectations that only cause further stress and anger. Internalizing anger predisposes a person to going off on others. Both perfectionism and internalizing anger increase tension and stress, which can eventually result in the IBW syndrome.

Health Signals

Some women initially have little awareness of the correlation between the Invincible Black Woman syndrome, stress, and physical ailments. Some early signals that let sisters know they are falling deeper into the IBW syndrome include headaches. Ignoring headaches as a warning signal of the IBW syndrome can lead to further physical ailments because we are ignoring our body's internal message. Rebecca, whom we met in Chapter 2, didn't pay attention to the early signals that she received when she had headaches on a daily basis. Eventually she started feeling a shortness of breath and tightness in her chest. She went to the emergency room thinking that she was having a heart attack but the doctors informed her that she was suffering from stress and anxiety. The body can give women numerous early warning signals that tell us we are in the IBW syndrome, and there are plenty of ways that women can respond to help themselves, which will be discussed later in this chapter and also in Chapter 10.

Negative Self-Talk

Negative self-talk is a pessimistic internal conversation that some women have while experiencing the IBW syndrome. Negative self-talk often comes in the form of anxiety, such as having an internal dialogue in which you are convinced that people are talking about you or do not like you. Rebecca thought that her friends gossiped about her after she had a baby. She was relying on negative gut feelings; "No one told me that anyone was talking about me behind my back, I just had a feeling that they were." Rebecca erroneously acted upon those negative gut feelings. When a girlfriend admitted that she was not ready to have children or a serious relationship, Rebecca believed this comment was a subtle implication that her friend was criticizing her for being a single mom.

Negative internal thoughts led Rebecca to interpret comments that others made as a direct insult to her situation. She stopped speaking to her friends and lost a support network that could have prevented her from falling deeper into the IBW syndrome. Developing an awareness of the frequency with which you carry on negative self-talk dialogue is another way to identify when you are in the IBW syndrome. Countering the negative internal conversation is essential to helping sisters understand how they have contributed to their own anxiety.

Perfectionistic Tendencies

When women place unrealistic expectations on themselves, it is characteristic of the middle phase of the IBW syndrome. Rebecca tried to present herself as the perfect mom and housekeeper after she thought others were talking about her. When friends called, she would say that she was busy cleaning the house or occupied with her son. Rebecca would struggle to portray the perfect mother and son relationship. She isolated her son from his relatives because she didn't want them to know that she did not receive child support. Rebecca recalled, "I needed shoes for my baby's feet and I was too ashamed to ask for help." Rebecca didn't want her relatives to begin asking questions about her son's father. Behind perfectionism are usually feelings of insecurity and a desire to avoid conflict with others. Try to replace perfectionistic behaviors with realistic behaviors.

Internalizing Anger

Failure to express anger often leads to depression in the final stages of the IBW syndrome. Adrian suspected that her husband Cecil, a computer programmer, was cheating on her because he spent most of his free time during the evenings "surfing" Internet chat rooms. Cecil would also travel alone for weekend outings. Adrian internalized her anger toward Cecil and she lost interest in sexual pleasure with him. Feeling depressed, she began to cry often and substitute food for comfort, gaining thirty pounds. After the weight gain, Adrian would look in the mirror and tell herself that she hated the way that she looked. Internalizing anger fuels a continual state of anxiety and guilt. Also included in the blueprint of internalized anger are self-destructive behaviors such as drug abuse and physical ailments. In the IBW syndrome, internalizing anger is the final stage before going off.

Going Off

Internalizing anger predisposes women to go off on others. In the IBW syndrome, going off is a buildup of internalized anger over a period of time. Adrian went off on Cecil after she internalized her anger about their relationship. Adrian's suspicions lead her to retrieve an e-mail that Cecil forwarded to another woman. Initially, instead of confronting Cecil about the e-mail, she began complaining about the amount of time that he spent on the computer. Adrian couldn't contain her secret any longer; she told

Cecil that she knew about the e-mail. She lost control and went off, called him names, and slapped him in the face. Cecil made an emergency appointment for marital therapy: "I have to make an appointment to see a therapist right away for myself and my wife because now she's hitting me." Going off on others is not a productive way for women to express their anger because it does not allow them to take responsibility for their feelings. Adrian could not communicate her feelings to Cecil until she entered into marital therapy. During therapy sessions, Adrian and Cecil had to follow rules for communication while discussing their issues. Neither of them were allowed to make accusations or call names. They had to focus on expressing their own feelings. At home, Adrian stopped hitting Cecil and they began to communicate more effectively. When Adrian stopped going off on Cecil she was able to discuss the real issues at hand and avoid potentially explosive behavior.

HOW DO I DISTINGUISH WHEN I'M IN THE IBW SYNDROME AND WHEN I'M NOT?

When we begin to tell ourselves the truth about what heals and what hurts, we can identify when we're in the IBW syndrome and when we are not. We need to listen to the intuitive gifts that we have been given as women to clarify our needs. How often do we actually evaluate ourselves and the decisions that we make? We wonder how we get ourselves into situations because we do things others ask us to do without thinking about our own needs. When we worry too much about pleasing others, we'll find we are exhibiting Invincible Woman tendencies. Figuring out when we are in the IBW syndrome is directly related to changing fantasy thoughts and negative thoughts into reality thoughts and positive thoughts. Sisters in the IBW syndrome often have negative thoughts. Sister Circle Note #1 suggested keeping a journal to record your moods. Note the frequency of negative thinking in your journal. The following list demonstrates how to counter negative internal dialogue with reality statements:

1. I MUST DO WHAT OTHERS WANT ME TO DO.

    It is a fantasy to think that you can please everyone in all that you do.

2. I HAVE TO ACT LIKE I'M INVINCIBLE.

    Everyone has peaks and valleys in their life. How we cope with the highs and lows is most important.

3. I NEVER DO ANYTHING RIGHT.

    Never is an all-encompassing term. It is important to give yourself credit for your accomplishments.

4. I'M NOT GOOD ENOUGH.

    Respecting yourself is the first step toward accepting yourself. Spend some time identifying your desired goals.

5. I'M ALONE AND NO ONE CARES ABOUT ME.

    Negative behavior patterns can affect relationships. Consider counseling to establish a therapeutic relationship and develop appropriate communication skills.

ACKNOWLEDGE FEELINGS OF POWERLESSNESS

Sisters experiencing the IBW syndrome usually struggle to break free from it. When women acknowledge feelings of powerlessness, they are in a crisis that has finally reached an overwhelming level. Women in this situation are pushed to the limit and feel an urgent need to decrease their anxiety. As a result of this, sisters are motivated to alleviate this feeling of being in the IBW syndrome and are more open to changing the way they have been behaving and thinking.

STEPS TO RECOVERY

In the spirit of Fannie Lou Hamer's famous quote, "I'm sick and tired of being sick and tired," sisters must stand up for themselves in order to break out of the syndrome. They must argue for their rights. Keep in mind the Sister Circle Bill of Rights on the following page as you read through the practical steps that lead to renewal, balance, and recovery from the IBW syndrome.

Identify Stressors

When feeling overwhelmed with stress, one of the first steps toward taking responsibility for what is happening in your life is to identify your stressors. Identifying stressors means discovering stressful situations in your life and how to gain control over them. The following five steps can help to identify stressors:

1. EXAMINE YOUR EMOTIONAL SIGNS.
   Review the IBW syndrome chart on page 148. Do you have any of these symptoms? Do you go off?

2. IDENTIFY YOUR BEHAVIORAL SIGNS.
   Do you have any compulsive behaviors such as spending, eating, sex, or substance abuse? Do you have difficulty with controlling aggressive tendencies? Are you constantly late to work? Do you exhibit avoidance behavior?

THE SISTER CIRCLE BILL OF RIGHTS

1. I have the right to have peace and time alone.

2. I have the right to unequivocally express my womanhood.

3. I have the right to acknowledge that I am angry with someone I love.

4. I have the right to say "no" to special favors or requests that I cannot meet.

5. I have the right to make my own decisions.

6. I have the right to say, "I'm not invincible."

7. I have the right to be treated fairly and with respect.

8. I have the right to feel good about who I am.

9. I have the right to enjoy myself and feel happy.

10. I have the right to hold fast to my dreams, values, and beliefs.

3. **ACKNOWLEDGE THE PROBLEM.**

What are the contributing factors that generate feelings of anger or sadness? What problems are you in denial about that lead to the IBW syndrome?

4. ANALYZE THE ISSUES.

Clarify your issues by writing them down on paper. Identify who is involved or affected.

5. PRIORITIZE THE ISSUES.

Prioritize the issues that bother you most. Identify your needs and the needs of those involved.

Seek Counseling and Self-Help Regimens

Counseling and self-help regimens can encourage an awareness of feelings and facilitate effective problem solving. Monica, a career mom with a preschooler, complained of feeling overwhelmed when she received a promotion. "I had a preschooler at home, a husband who traveled often, deadlines at work, and I had to begin training my replacement." Monica was a career woman and wife who wanted to focus on building relationships with her child and her husband. She was especially interested in involving her daughter in activities outside the home. Monica had a routine of working long hours, caring for her preschooler, and assuming major responsibility for the home. When Monica found it impossible to work and take care of her family, she began to complain and have heated arguments with her husband about it. She would tell him, "I'm tired of all this pressure that you are putting on me. You don't appreciate me." They both agreed to begin marital and family counseling.

Faced with conflicting demands on her time, Monica did not fall into the Invincible Black Woman syndrome trap. Instead of placing unnecessary stress on herself and denying her feelings, Monica began listening to her anger and using language that identified and focused on her needs. Monica began this introspection through homework assignments that she received in counseling.

INVINCIBLE BLACK WOMAN SYNDROME SCALE

INTENSITY

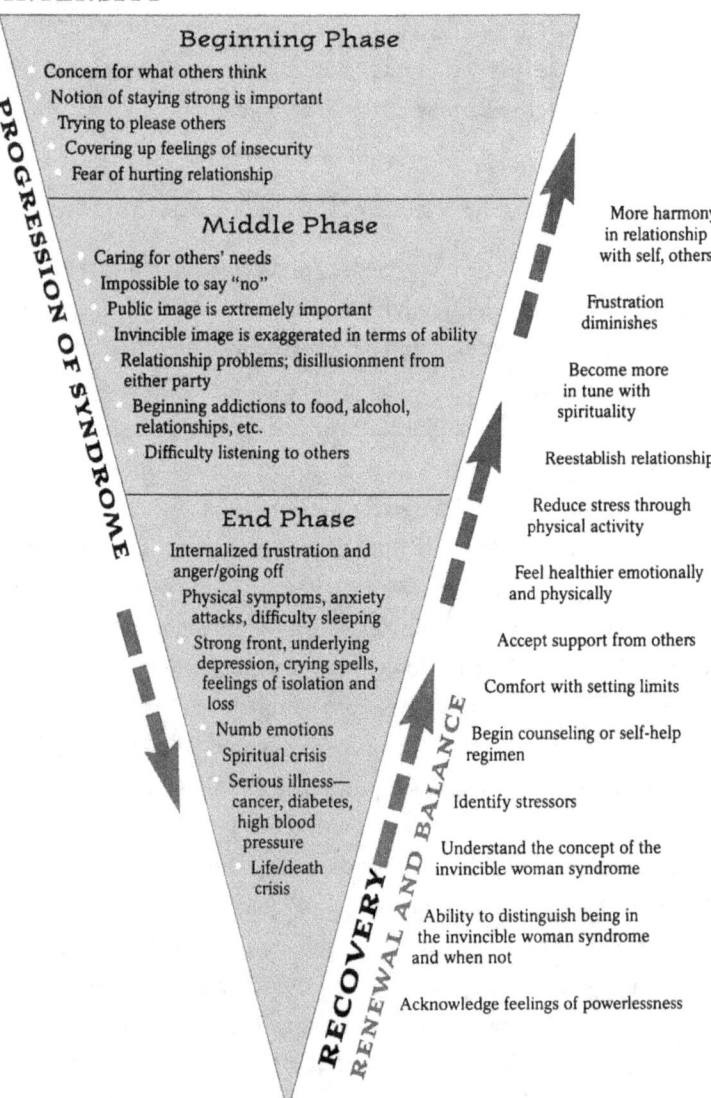

Beginning Phase

- Concern for what others think
- Notion of staying strong is important
- Trying to please others
- Covering up feelings of insecurity
- Fear of hurting relationship

Middle Phase

- Caring for others' needs
- Impossible to say "no"
- Public image is extremely important
- Invincible image is exaggerated in terms of ability
- Relationship problems; disillusionment from either party
- Beginning addictions to food, alcohol, relationships, etc.
- Difficulty listening to others

End Phase

- Internalized frustration and anger/going off
- Physical symptoms, anxiety attacks, difficulty sleeping
- Strong front, underlying depression, crying spells, feelings of isolation and loss
- Numb emotions
- Spiritual crisis
- Serious illness— cancer, diabetes, high blood pressure
- Life/death crisis

PROGRESSION OF SYNDROME

RECOVERY, RENEWAL AND BALANCE

More harmony in relationship with self, others

Frustration diminishes

Become more in tune with spirituality

Reestablish relationships

Reduce stress through physical activity

Feel healthier emotionally and physically

Accept support from others

Comfort with setting limits

Begin counseling or self-help regimen

Identify stressors

Understand the concept of the invincible woman syndrome

Ability to distinguish being in the invincible woman syndrome and when not

Acknowledge feelings of powerlessness

Then she began by telling her husband, "I am feeling extremely stressed with managing my career, taking care of our child, and cleaning the house. I need to do something about this problem and I'm asking for your support." Through discussions, they made a list of priorities for the house and decided that if they were to live the way they wanted to live, they would have to find outside help. Monica and her husband hired a cleaning service on a weekly basis to help her with the house cleaning. The time she normally spent cleaning was then available for her to spend with her daughter.

Writing Through Pain

Rebecca acknowledged her feelings of powerlessness by writing them down. She had a health crisis during the final stages she experienced in the IBW syndrome. When she thought that she was having a heart attack, she was consumed with anger, frustration, fear, and confusion. Worst of all, she felt alone and isolated. She thought that if she wrote down her feelings, she'd feel better. Writing down her feelings was not an easy task to perform. Many times she had a piece of paper and pen ready and she was afraid to confront her emotions. Her emotions felt so powerful that when she tried to express them she became overwhelmed. Rebecca would begin to write and start crying instead. Then, when she reached her wits' end, she started writing. Her emotions poured through her and she felt a sense of relief and some alleviation from her pain.

Rebecca's repressed feelings began to resurface from the dread of having to take her son to the emergency room again when his asthma grew increasingly worse. After a series of bad experiences, Rebecca lacked confidence in the medical system. She didn't know if she could trust the advice of the doctors and nurses and she wanted to get a second opinion about the instructions and medications they prescribed. She wondered if better treatment was available elsewhere. It even felt like the hospital staff in the emergency room treated her with indifference after she informed them that she did not have insurance coverage. When she really needed them to show some compassion, she was reminded about an outstanding balance. Rebecca spent hours in the emergency room before her son was seen. A staff person referred them for follow-up with their family doctor without administering any treatment for her son's asthma condition. Rebecca did not want her son to witness their refusal to treat him at the emergency room again. She attempted to see a family doctor for a checkup for herself as well as her son and was refused treatment again because she had outstanding medical bills and no insurance.

Finally, when Rebecca's boyfriend left her, she felt unable to cope with any more rejection or pain. In the end, Rebecca was so overwhelmed, depressed, and desperate with the job of maintaining her strong front that she pulled out her writing again, and sent it to a newspaper editor to share her pain with complete strangers. Initially, Rebecca didn't write her story for the newspaper. One of the newspaper editors called her to make sure that she wasn't going to commit suicide and to tell her that her essay would be printed in the Saturday evening edition. "After my story appeared," Rebecca said, "I received sympathetic calls and letters from women of all walks of life. Those who had had similar experiences understood my anger, in particular, as they knew where I had been and what this kind of anger can do."

Feel Comfort with Setting Limits

Taking on too many responsibilities that infringe on your work or leisure time can create irritability and frustration. Women in the IBW syndrome have to learn to say "no" to additional responsibilities. Often, women are unrealistic about how much they can accomplish in a day. The following tips can help you feel more productive and provide stress relief:

1. Prioritize your duties by making daily "to do" lists. Forecast your priorities on a weekly and monthly basis for increased efficiency.
2. Think about how much you can achieve from a realistic point of view.
3. Identify peak energy periods, for example, mornings or evenings, and plan to complete your most demanding task during this time.
4. Avoid Invincible Black Woman perfectionistic tendencies and focus on obtaining the required results.
5. Evaluate your work and delegate tasks to the appropriate persons.
6. Utilize decision-making skills to eliminate wasting time.
7. Take time to work uninterrupted in the office and at home when focusing on a project.
8. Take a positive approach toward work responsibilities.
9. Set goals and review them periodically. Recognize your accomplishments.
10. Allow time for self, family, and leisure activities.

Accept Support from Others

Overcompensating, women in the IBW syndrome avoid confronting their problems and are less likely to seek support from others. When Rebecca wrote about her pain to the local newspaper, her phone rang off the hook. Her friends were surprised, not knowing how vulnerable she had been. Rebecca continued to receive support from others in the form of letters, cards, poetry, and gifts for nearly a year. She carried her letters and cards around in a tote bag and read them periodically to make her feel better. Due to these letters of encouragement, Rebecca began to feel empowered, and her situation began to change. A woman who worked in the credit department of the hospital told hospital administrators that Rebecca's article generated negative publicity, and they decided to write off all of her outstanding medical bills based on lack of insurance coverage and low income status. An employer responded to Rebecca's article by offering her a full-time job with medical benefits, which she accepted. Rebecca commented, "I feel better both mentally and physically. Now when things build up, I write to vent my feelings and I belong to a support group." Social support systems help alleviate the pressures of everyday life.

Reduce Stress: Emotional and Physical Health

Developing a plan for emotional and physical health is key for stress reduction. Cherone, a single mother, had her first child at the age of twenty-two, and, to her dismay, she could not seem to lose the weight she gained while pregnant. Meanwhile, Cherone was angry because her boyfriend, John, stopped paying attention to her and never complimented her. "I felt powerless because I couldn't get rid of the weight. I couldn't seem to control it. I was feeling trapped at home with the baby because I wanted to work and attend college. I was angry about my situation and began to cry often. Food made me feel so much better and when I cooked, sometimes John would come around to visit."

Cherone's sense of anger and frustration increased, and she continued to gain more and more weight. John took to making fun of her weight and to snatching food from her hand. Her physician called her "obese" as her weight hit two hundred pounds. Feeling devastated, Cherone started to turn inward, exhibiting symptoms of the IBW syndrome. Cherone developed a negative self-image and said hurtful things to herself. She allowed food to become a source of comfort for stress reduction.

Cherone's self-destructive behavior continued until she was hospitalized with a potentially life-threatening condition caused by her overeating. She was diagnosed with diabetes and high blood pressure. Her doctor warned that she could eventually suffer heart and kidney problems.

Following her diagnosis, Cherone began to take nutrition classes to learn how to plan her diabetic meals. After consulting with her doctor Cherone began an exercise program and started to feel better and lose weight. Cherone learned that she could feel good about herself without expecting any validation from a man. Cherone commented, "John is still my boyfriend; however, he is only one aspect of my life. I have learned that my health and well-being is most important and that I must take care of myself and my child first."

Developing a plan to feel better emotionally and physically requires making a personal commitment. After having a checkup from your physician regarding any physical exercise precautions, we recommend the following activities:

1. JOURNAL WRITING.

   As previously mentioned, use a journal to write about your thoughts and feelings. If you have a problem that needs to be addressed, start writing. Writing serves as a form of release when you're angry and can reduce the urge to go off on others.

2. DEVELOP AN EXERCISE ROUTINE.

   Simply start by walking. There may be a walking group in your neighborhood that you can join. Consult with a personal trainer for a customized exercise plan.

3. ENJOY A HEALTHY DIET.

   Think of eating nutrients as a pleasure for the body. Ration your meat portions and pick vibrantly colored fruits and vegetables like yams, greens, tomatoes, and red peppers. Soul food ought to be food that has sustenance for the body *and* soul.

4. MONITOR YOUR SLEEP AND REST.

   Are you getting enough sleep? How do you relax? Take an inventory of your sleep and rest patterns to ensure that they are adequate.

5. UTILIZE RELAXATION TECHNIQUES.

   Relaxation techniques can help reduce stress and body tension. Consider practicing the following deep breathing exercise:

   - Sit in a comfortable position.
   - With your eyes closed, focus on your breathing process.
   - While concentrating on your breathing, allow your breathing to flow in and out of your body.
   - Meditate on these thoughts: "I will let my breathing flow smoothly in and out of my body. My breathing

is like rhythm in motion. I feel at peace and rejuve-
nated."

- Continue breathing in rhythmic flow, and concen-
trate on your breathing process.
- After approximately five minutes, stretch, stand, and
continue with your daily schedule.

Reestablish Relationships

Reestablishing relationships that you have neglected or avoided
because of anger and resentment can be beneficial to your health
and recovery from the IBW syndrome. It is important to consider
a cooperative approach, because maybe both of you have valid
issues to discuss. Angie, whom we discussed in Chapter 3, became
estranged from her sister Arlene after her mother died. Angie
became pregnant but she had a boyfriend who was noncommittal.
She decided to handle the pregnancy and rearing of her child by
herself. While at the hospital for a routine checkup, she was asked
to take a test for HIV. Angie was not going to take the test, but
decided that it wouldn't hurt her if she took it, so she agreed. Her
test results came back HIV positive. "I was angry. I am through
with men! Through with them! It was not like I was some ho out
there screwing guys. I had two or three dates over the past year
and I don't know who gave it to me. The health department no-
tified the father of my baby. Now I have three kids, one who
might be HIV positive, and I don't know how to tell my sister,
but I have to because I want her to take care of my kids when
I'm gone."

Angie is concerned for her baby, praying that each test the
baby takes for HIV is negative. How Angie spiritually dealt with
her situation is discussed in Chapter 10.

■　■　■

ACKNOWLEDGING WHEN YOU are in the IBW syndrome and identifying your issues can help you move through the path of recovery from the syndrome with ease. Breaking out of the syndrome can result in a healthier sense of self and well being. You improve your outlook as well as have more meaningful relationships with those around you. The final key to maintaining balance and complete recovery is through peace and spirituality, which is discussed in Chapter 10.

1O SPIRITUAL RELEASE

"Yes, it's okay to cry because tears make you whole.
They're a libation to the spirit, a washing of the
soul, a renewal."

—QUEEN AFUA, *THE SACRED WOMAN*

OUR INCREASING RELIANCE ON technology contributes to the IBW syndrome, depression, and going off. With
advances in technology, there are more conveniences than ever
before to make our homes more comfortable. Computers and the
Internet offer us the world at our fingertips. We can keep in touch
with one another at all times through cellular phones, pagers, and
other data devices. All of these conveniences are supposed to
make life easier, but simultaneously, they make it more difficult.
Women find more ways to confirm their suspicions about men by
tracking them down with every electronic device available.

Sierra realized that she got along much better with her boyfriend when she didn't call him on his cell phone and pager
throughout the day: "I really didn't need to call him five or six
times a day. He was becoming a little annoyed with me and the
mystique about me that attracted him in the first place was disappearing. I was becoming a person with no life other than to
track him down somewhere." With everything technology has to
offer, if we haven't connected with our spiritual path, we are at

risk of feeling empty with a profound sense of loss that often leads to anger and depression.

CONNECT WITH YOUR SPIRITUAL PATH

Increasing spirituality requires time alone, which we often try to avoid. Solitude can teach us to validate ourselves and satisfy our needs, providing us with time to stop listening to the voices of people who think they know what's best for us. Time spent alone can help us restore the energy that we give to everyone else. Spiritual time helps us pull out of Invincible Black Women tendencies, and it allows us to recover from stress. We are often so busy taking care of others that we forget to honor ourselves. Take a long look in the mirror. What do you tell yourself when you look in the mirror? Do you like what you see? Tell yourself to accept and feel good about who you are. Dedicate time to relax and replenish your mind and body.

RITUALS STRENGTHEN SPIRITUAL LIFE

Rituals encourage us to return to the four elements of nature—earth, air, fire, and water—which were used by our ancestors for blessings and sacred events. Rituals restore a sense of balance amid the chaos while also giving greater purpose and meaning to our lives. They allow us to take a step back, reflect, and relax. They can also help us to release some of our anger or depression. Memories from rituals are significant reminders that help keep us on the right course. They represent a commitment to self-

SISTER CIRCLE NOTE #10

Daily devotions help strengthen spiritual life.
When you want to go off, don't go there! Listen to
the Creator and gain wisdom.

*I will make a commitment to practice daily prayer and
meditation in my life.*

READ: PROVERBS 15:1–7

improvement as well as honoring and respecting our contribution
to the earth.

Rituals for Life-Changing Transitions

Angie, the HIV positive mother mentioned earlier, needed a life-transforming ritual after losing her mother and contracting HIV. Prayer and the ritual with her women's circle from the AIDS Work Force helped Angie to overcome anger about her condition. She felt comfortable around her sister circle but she hid her medical condition from her family. "I'm worried and full of anxiety about telling my family that I'm HIV positive," Angie confessed. She discussed how to deal with the anxiety with her women's circle.

She decided to gain strength and courage by honoring her life transition with a ritual. Angie prepared for this ritual by selecting traditional African clothing. These articles of clothing made her feel a connection to her family as well as her African ancestors.

She also selected seven aromatic candles for the seven members of her women's circle attending the ceremony. For herself, Angie selected three bone bead candleholders, two of the same height and one higher to represent the Holy Trinity. On the day of the ritual, Angie fasted and prayed. With support group members surrounding her, Angie sat in the middle of the circle with unlit candles all around her. Each member brought with them a polished stone that symbolized a good quality, such as patience. Angie also wore a scarf that her deceased mother had given to her, as a blessing to represent healing.

Each woman approached Angie, telling of her own ordeal of living with HIV, and offered her a gift. They each started with "My sister, I give you a gift of . . ." When Angie received the gift, she responded with, "My sister, I accept your gift of healing, peace, patience, and bless you with light." Angie then lit a candle and gave it to the woman who had given her the gift. Group members lit Angie's three candles from their candles and blessed her. At the close of the rite, the group hugged one another, blew out the candles and took them home. The candles were to be lit again on the following day when Angie was scheduled to meet with her family to inform them about her condition. All circle members agreed to fast and pray on the day of Angie's family meeting. The rite gave Angie the courage to break her silence and notify her family members of her condition. Angie feels that through prayer she was able to gain the strength to share her heartbreak, reconnect with purpose and meaning in her life, and move on. No longer feeling alone in a world where she felt no one cared, Angie became an advocate for other women with HIV and AIDS. Her baby has not tested HIV positive, and Angie is thankful. She takes one day at a time, and enjoys the life and renewed sense of being that she has to share with her children.

Rituals for Recovery from Sexual Assault

Diane, a forty-three-year-old administrator, had been molested by her father. She had a negative image of her body and did not enjoy her sexuality. She had been in therapy for six months. "I need to feel my rage and reclaim my power," Diane lamented to her therapist. For years she had been reliving the abuse and had had many crises. She needed to create a rite for her recovery from the incest to reclaim her body and her life.

To prepare for her ritual, Diane wrote a poem to symbolize a new beginning in her life. She painted a vase to represent her body and surrounded the vase with fresh roses. The roses symbolized peace, love, beauty, and unfolding. Next to the vase she had a pitcher of water to represent cleansing, passion, and a new beginning. She laid these items in front of the fireplace. A log sat next to the fireplace. A candle sat on top of the fireplace. Her husband supported her during the ritual. Diane started the ritual by yelling, "Get off of me! Go away! Stop! . . ." She picked up the log which represented her father, and placed it in the fireplace. After she lit the log, she read her poem as her husband poured water into the vase. Together, they filled the vase with roses. Diane lit the candle and they prayed together. After the ritual was over, tears streamed down both of their faces as they blew out the candle and embraced one another.

Gwyn, a massage therapist and yoga teacher, was raised by an aunt and uncle because her parents abandoned her. She was raped at the age of twelve, and as a result gave birth to a daughter. Her aunt and uncle assisted Gwyn for a few years, but after she turned sixteen Gwyn raised her daughter alone. Although she had a tremendous amount of anger about the rape and the subsequent responsibilities of an unwanted pregnancy and raising a young child alone, Gwyn did not remain a bitter person. "I had to get beyond that anger," she said. "I had to go beyond my fear." Gwyn's personal ritual is practicing yoga and prayer. Through regularly performing this ritual she feels that the power and presence of God was always there for her and she has found a tremendous inspiration in that fact. She continued, "I came to see that I am one with everybody, and the isolation I had felt previously was just leading to more anger and jealousy."

The power to rid ourselves of anger and blame lies within us when we discover the higher self, or that spiritual part of us that doesn't allow us to dwell on negativity and anger. The higher self takes us to another level of existence where we are more aligned with the harmonious flow of the universe, where our feelings of peace, joy, and love are heightened. When we reach this place within ourselves, we can begin to listen to our intuitions and clarify our needs.

A Ritual for Letting Go

Jessica, the computer programmer from Chapter 7, had quit her job because of frustration, anger, and lack of recognition. After she quit, she was still angry with her former employer and often replayed the turn of events in her mind. She didn't have another job lined up, and she didn't want to accept another job without careful consideration of her career direction. She was not happy in her last position, and she did not want to repeat the same path. She had to let go; it was time for a career change. Since graduation from college, she had been working as a computer programmer for five years. She had worked long hours and never had much time to reflect on her career goals.

After meeting with a career counselor, she made a decision to start her own business. She wanted to design Web pages and operate her own Web site. To help her transition, she invited her inner circle of friends to support her by attending her "coming out" party. Setting up a ritual was important because it enabled her to address the fears from the past as well as her hopes for the future. She chose yellow candles to symbolize her transformation, a plant with blooming flowers to symbolize roots and a new beginning, and her new business logo to symbolize identification with her new career. She asked each of her friends to write or bring something to share about their careers or career aspirations as well.

After dinner, they sat around the dining room and began to share their stories. She began the ritual by lighting the candles and telling her circle about her new business. She discussed her previous painful employment experiences and unveiled her new logo. She thanked her friends for their support. After the event, she received several calls from her friends as well as referrals to design Web sites. As uncertain as she had been about self-employment, the ritual served as a motivational force to help her release the past and move on with a new beginning. With her spare time, Jessica consults with other businesses and feels that she is serving her purpose in life.

A Celebration Ritual

Ali, the frustrated retail salesperson from Chapter 2, fell into the IBW syndrome after deferring her dream of becoming a professional singer to take care of her family. Ali began to wonder whether she'd ever begin to take vocal lessons or join a choir. What stressed her out most was the fact that she wasn't getting any younger, and with each birthday her goal seemed farther out of reach. Wrestling with her age verses her goals, she decided to stop fighting her age because it was inevitable.

Turning thirty-five signaled a new stage in Ali's growth and development. She decided to pray for direction in her life and began to read daily devotions. Her spiritual development strengthened as she faced the changes that were about to occur in her life. Her family seemed more in tune with one another and the children were helping around the house more often. Ali felt that it was a perfect moment in her life to select a special ritual.

Ali was living in North Carolina and she enjoyed the warm weather in the spring. This year, on her birthday, the weather was especially warm and she decided to spend her birthday in the mountains where she could have a private atmosphere for meditation and time alone with her family.

She rented a villa that had a fireplace upstairs and a whirlpool tub in the master bath. Ali decided to take a walk in honor of her birthday. As she walked, she practiced deep breathing techniques. She walked along the nature trail and enjoyed the fresh air. When she returned to the villa, she lit candles and took a whirlpool bath. As she meditated in the warm, bubbly, and refreshing water she felt a spiritual uplift. She was beginning to perceive herself as a tenacious person that *could* become a gospel singer. She softly hummed tunes and realized that music was within her if only she would be still and listen.

After her bath, Ali met her family by the fireplace. A sense of calm and peace had come over her. She lit the fireplace, and as she gazed in the fire she reflected on her walk and the refreshing bath. Ali thanked her family for honoring her wish to spend some time alone. She discussed her thoughts about wanting to be a gospel singer and began to sing for her family. Her children had never seen her so happy and they enjoyed her gift of song. Her family offered their support of her desire to change careers. She ended the ritual for her birthday celebration by saying a prayer before blowing out the candles on her cake.

ANGER IN DREAMS

You should learn to interpret your anger dreams because they are messages from your hidden self to your conscious self. This self-knowledge is essential if you want to become a happy, well-adjusted woman. The dream might be an attempt by your subconscious to bring to your awareness some unfinished business about your anger. If you ignore the dream, the communication is lost.

The earliest record of how dreams direct our actions are in the Bible. In Genesis, the story of Joseph reveals how his life was shaped by a dream that he experienced at the age of seventeen. Joseph's dreams became a life-changing force that helped his family escape famine and death.

The two most recognized dream theorists are Sigmund Freud and his associate Carl Gustav Jung. Freud believed that dreams were presentations of repressed desires, usually sexual in nature. He suggested that they had a manifest content (what occurred in the dream) and a latent content (what the dream tries to tell us).

Jung believed that dreams are the voice of the unconscious mind. For example, during waking hours we may not continue arguments through to their logical conclusions, especially if the talk is heading toward disaster. We may prefer to forget the whole matter, which can bring about disturbing results in our emotional lives. However, analyzing a dream can bring hidden meaning to light. We may discover that we need to look deeply into a situation in a way that we had not considered while awake.

Recording your anger dreams will help you to recognize any recurring patterns that appear in your dreams. Keep a notepad at your bedside so you can make notes about your dream when you wake up. Later, transfer your notes and any additional vivid memories about your dream to a journal. On the left-hand side of your page, write a narrative of the dream; on the right-hand side, write your interpretation. Include your emotions in your interpretation and what may have triggered your anger dream. Give your dream a title. Anger can express itself in our dreams through strong emotional reactions and verbal and physical interactions. These types of dreams may continue until you recognize the source of your anger dream and deal with it.

Ritual for Anger in Dreams

Rochelle, a thirty-four-year-old secretary, recalled experiencing anger in a dream. At the time of the dream, Rochelle was angry with her sister Connie, but unable to express her feelings to her sibling. The cause of her anger was Connie's engagement to a con artist who had been in prison. When Rochelle discovered that Connie's fiancé, Phil, had given Connie a stolen engagement ring, Rochelle was angry with Connie for overlooking Phil's suspicious behavior. Rochelle feared that if she confronted Connie about Phil, Connie wouldn't believe her and it would only draw her closer to Phil. Here is Rochelle's dream: "I finally told her how stupid she was regarding Phil. I told her that he was a con artist and had no good intentions for her. I was yelling at Connie, and we began to fight."

When Rochelle's daughter woke her from her dream, Rochelle was standing up, yelling, and swinging in the air. The dream prompted Rochelle to speak directly with her sister. At that time, Connie admitted that she was beginning to have her doubts about Phil. Together, Connie and Rochelle decided to perform a ritual about Rochelle's dream. First, Rochelle wrote down everything that she could remember about her dream. Next, they began to do some research for the ritual. Rochelle researched information on Phil through the county sheriff's office Web site on the Internet. Phil was listed as one of the area's most wanted for grand theft. Rochelle printed his picture and criminal record. Both Rochelle and Connie wrote a script for the ritual. Rochelle wrote about feeling like Connie was a part of herself in the dream. Connie wrote a goodbye letter to Phil. The sisters held the ritual at the dining room table. Rochelle placed the criminal profile of Phil on the table and Connie set her letter on top of Rochelle's paper. Rochelle lit a candle and Connie tearfully read her goodbye letter. Connie took off her engagement ring after reading the letter and enclosed it in an envelope together with the other papers. Together, they blew out the candle. This restored harmony between Rochelle and Connie. Afterward, they mailed the package to Phil and he did not contact Connie again.

Diane, the woman who suffered from sexual assault, had a recurring dream: "I was in a courtroom. He was seated in a chair and the trial was about to begin. I was feeling intense anger." Diane's dream only had a beginning, never an ending. The dream symbolized the anger and frustration that came from wanting to punish her father for what he had done to her. She remembers the shocking night when she was fourteen, and he came into her room, unzipped his pants, and forced her legs open. As he forced himself into her, she fainted. At times Diane would become consumed with anger in her waking adult life. One night she became so angry that she loaded a gun and drove around looking for her father in the bars he frequented. She didn't find him that night, but she believed that if she had she would have killed him. That's when she decided along with her therapist to perform a ritual about her dream. Diane decided to perform her ritual with her husband. Diane recalled her dream from memory and from her notes in her journal and wrote a script. Diane played the role of the judge and her husband played the role of her father. She cut out paper handcuffs and had an orange T-shirt for her husband to wear. Diane's husband responded to her questions according to her script. Diane pronounced her father guilty. The two of them sat in silence together. Diane could feel the dream made real in her spirit. Justice had been served.

In waking life, going off may temporarily serve as a release but, as mentioned earlier, it usually makes a situation worse. If you dream of going off or verbally abusing someone, your dream may be telling you that you haven't dealt with a problem. If you use weapons in a dream, then your anger may have reached a dangerous state. If you are threatening or attacking a person in a dream, then you may feel hostility for that person in waking life.

LETTING GO AND LOOKING IN

When you honor yourself, you will start to let go and take care of yourself in the same way that you have taken care of others. Learn to let go of distractions that contribute to angry feelings and develop self-love and self-nurturing. Pay attention to your feelings, thoughts, and actions to help you grow spiritually. When anger is triggered, think beyond simple acts like going off and discern what you're responding to.

Consider ten tips for looking in instead of lashing out. Facilitate the process of letting go.

1. TAKE TIME OUT FOR YOURSELF.

   At work, take a five to fifteen minute break to release tension and nervousness. Include a stretch, desk exercises, and walking.

2. LET GO OF THE INVINCIBLE BLACK WOMAN COMPLETELY.

   You have been holding in anger and letting go at the wrong time. Work on solving your problems instead of emphasizing and supporting your image of the Invincible Black Woman.

3. SEEK A FEMALE SUPPORT PERSON.

   Choose a sister with whom you can establish a positive relationship.

4. TALK TO A MENTAL HEALTH PROFESSIONAL.

   Sisters are often reluctant to see a therapist. Locate a therapist who is culturally competent and specializes in women's counseling so that you will have an opportunity to talk confidentially to someone who understands your situation.

5. CHECK YOURSELF.

   Look for things you are telling yourself that make you angry. For example, look for the use of words such as "always," "never," and "must." For example: "He always finds something wrong with my work," or "I will never find another job."

6. EXPLORE THE SELF-HELP AND PSYCHOLOGY SECTION OF THE LOCAL LIBRARY.

   The best-sellers' lists are a great reference source for useful books on these topics.

7. REPEAT AN AFFIRMATION THAT INSPIRES YOU.

   Affirmations counter the negative thoughts that anger cultivates. If you don't have a favorite affirmation, select one below:

   I am one with God.
   I respect and honor my feminine power.
   I believe in myself.
   I know I can.
   I am upset, and I am still okay.
   I know that this too will pass.
   I am blessed.
   I am a free spirit, ready to soar.
   I know myself and accept who I am.
   I will take one day at a time.

8. FOCUS ON SPIRITUAL DEVELOPMENT AND A POSITIVE ENVIRONMENT FOR SPIRITUAL SUPPORT.

   Begin by establishing a personal or family altar in your home.

9. PRACTICE RELAXATION AND BREATHING.

   Calm breathing helps to integrate the body, spirit, and mind. Close your eyes and fill your abdomen and lungs with an intake of air. Visualize the air as a pleasant, calming breeze from the sea. As you release the air, feel it cleanse your spirit while it brings harmony to your body and mind.

I 0. TRY AFFIRMATIVE BREATHING.

Remember, you have the power to change negative thoughts. Affirmative breathing can help ease your triggers. When negative thoughts creep in, take a breath and change to a positive thought.

FORGIVENESS

Mary, the dispatcher who wanted to become a firefighter, is now a firefighter with fourteen years on the job. She is and always has been the only woman to work at the station. "I had to learn how to forgive," said Mary. "I have always been strong-willed and stubborn. I felt determined to not let my true feelings show. Not just to other people, but most of all to myself." Mary had wanted to be a firefighter from a young age. Determined that being a woman would not stand in her way, she went through written examinations as well as a rigorous physical test. "When I found out what would be required for the physical examination, I wasn't strong enough to move some of the weights, so I had to train for six months prior to taking the physical," she admitted. Mary cried tears of joy when she found out she passed the physical: "Many men fail that portion of the test, but I was in the best physical condition of my life." Mary's happiness faded after she was hired as a firefighter at a station filled with men who resented her presence. "I got called every foul name in the book," Mary said. "The training period was the roughest time in my life. When I passed the training, they tried to take away from what I had accomplished by calling me more names. I pretended that none of the name-calling bothered me. I also pretended that I wasn't bothered by the fact that in a dangerous situation, none of the men would trust me as a fellow firefighter."

Internalizing this situation affected Mary's health and her relationships with others when she was not on the job. Finally, she nearly collapsed from stress. "All along I had told myself that I wasn't going anywhere, and they could accept me or reject me; I was here for the duration. I was doing my twenty years and getting retirement. But you know, deep down inside, I didn't know if I could handle it. When I went into counseling and admitted that I didn't know if I could handle it—when I released that stress and pent-up anger—everything changed for me. I finally believed in myself."

Mary acknowledged feelings of powerlessness and developed an understanding of when to be strong and how to release pressure through therapy. She learned that pretending something isn't there doesn't make it disappear. It was more useful to her to analyze the situation, to see things clearly, and then to make a conscious effort to focus on her job and her determination to stay employed for twenty years. As she focused on what was important to her, she began to have less time and energy for negativity. Her hard feelings for her co-workers began to dissolve, as did her anger. She was letting go. Each time Mary let go of grudges, she grew stronger and more determined to stay at her job. Everything changed for her after that. As she let go, she began to forgive; as she forgave, she found it easier to let go. Instead of being an Invincible Black Woman who suffers from suppressed emotions and self-enforced control, Mary became a strong woman—a woman who could let go, forgive, understand, and take responsibility for her own emotions. In the process, Mary began to find some inner peace and happiness.

The act of forgiveness is one of the greatest ways to cleanse the spirit. Forgiveness can be taken on consciously as a sort of "spiritual vitamin" as we follow these steps:

1. Define the exact source of anger and pain.
2. Strive to understand what happened and why by determining the part you played in the scenario.
3. Initiate an inner dialogue of forgiveness to release the anger and begin the forgiving process.
4. Anticipate the relief you will feel by letting go.
5. Feel the peace.

A Ritual for Developing Forgiveness

Spend a few moments sitting quietly. Ask yourself if there is anyone you really dislike. Is there anyone you hate? Is there anyone with whom you have unresolved issues? Make a list of everyone throughout your life who has mistreated you, harmed you, or done you an injustice, or for whom you feel anger or hatred. Next to these names, write what they did to you or why you resent them.

Close your eyes and go through the list, one by one. Picture the person in front of you. Talk to him or her, explaining the feelings you have. Tell each one that you are now going to forgive him or her for everything. Let go. Forgive and release these people. Free yourself from the past and from the present connection that you have harbored through your negativity.

When you are finished, take the paper outside and burn it. As the paper turns to ashes, say, "I forgive you all. Today I am letting go of the past."

■ ■ ■

SISTERS ARE IN need of healing from emotional wounds from childhood traumas as well as stress from adulthood. Healing from anger is a good reason for performing a rite. We are a spiritual people and spirituality honors the sacredness within. If we use a clear mind to look at painful situations, we can see that discomfort is often a direct indicator that our experience contains a powerful lesson for us. Unpleasant as they may be, such lessons are necessary for personal growth. Going off and losing control can be our soul's way of getting our attention. When we go off, we are confronting our pain and responding to it. These are signals that change is needed in an area of our life. Health problems related to the IBW syndrome also offer warning signs that we need to change our coping mechanisms. By recognizing our triggers and behaviors we can reshape our perspective and ultimately respond better to situations.

APPENDIX

RECOMMENDED READING

BlackBoard 50 Best Books 2000

Disappearing Acts	Terry McMillan
Black Men: Obsolete, Single, Dangerous?	Haki R. Madhubuti
The Isis Papers	Frances Cress Welsing
The Autobiography of Malcolm X	Alex Haley
Their Eyes Were Watching God	Zora Neale Hurston
Jazz	Toni Morrison
Waiting to Exhale	Terry McMillan
Some Soul to Keep	J. California Cooper
Your Blues Ain't Like Mine	Bebe Moore Campbell
Visions For Black Men	Na'im Akbar
Erotique Noire: Black Erotica	Miriam DeCosta-Willis, Reginald Martin, Roseann P. Bell, eds.
The African American Holiday of Kwanzaa: A Celebration of Family, Community and Culture	Maulana Karenga
I Know Why the Caged Bird Sings	Maya Angelou
Jumping the Broom: The African-American Wedding Planner	Harriette Cole
Race Matters	Cornel West
I, Too, Sing America: The African Book of Days	Paula L. Woods, Felix H. Liddell
Nile Valley Contributions to Civilization	Anthony Browder
Black Pearls: Daily Meditations, Affirmations and Inspirations for African-Americans	Eric V. Copage

Volunteer Slavery: My Authentic Negro Experience	Jill Nelson
Ugly Ways	Tina McElroy Ansa
Having Our Say: The Delaney Sisters' *First 100 Years*	Sara L. and A. Elizabeth Delaney with Amy Hill Hearth
A Lesson Before Dying	Ernest J. Gains
In the Company of My Sisters: Black Women *and Self Esteem*	Julia A. Boyd
In the Spirit	Susan L. Taylor
The Original African Heritage Study Bible	Cain Hope Felder
Makes Me Wanna Holler: A Young Black Man *in America*	Nathan McCall
Coffee Will Make You Black	April Sinclair
Just as I Am	E. Lynn Harris
Sisters and Lovers	Connie Briscoe
Invisible Life	E. Lynn Harris
Devil in a Blue Dress	Walter Mosley
Success Runs in Our Race	George Fraser
Acts of Faith: Daily Meditations for People of Color	Iyanla Vanzant
The Personal Touch	Terrie Williams with Joe Cooney
"Why Should White Guys Have *All the Fun?"*	Reginald F. Lewis and Blair S. Walker
Body and Soul	Linda Villarosa, ed.
The Patternmaster	Octavia E. Butler
When Death Comes Stealing	Valerie Wilson Wesley
When We Were Colored	Clifton L. Taulbert
Tryin' to Sleep in the Bed You Made	Virginia DeBerry, Donna Grant
Don't Block the Blessings	Patti LaBelle with Laura B. Randolph
Friends and Lovers	Eric Jerome Dickey
In the Meantime: Finding Yourself and the *Love You Want*	Iyanla Vanzant

One Day My Soul Just Opened Up	Iyanla Vanzant
The Lady, Her Lover, and Her Lord	T. D. Jakes
Flyy Girl	Omar Tyree
On Air: The Best of Tavis Smiley on the Tom Joyner Show	Tavis Smiley
The Debt: What America Owes to Blacks	Randall Robinson

WEB SITES

www.blackexpressions.com: A virtual book club community. The official Web site for Black Expressions Book Club.

www.blackplanet.com: An informative African-American Web site: games, personal home pages, and more.

www.blackvoices.com: A favorite African-American Web site.

www.blackworld.com: A user-friendly Internet directory.

www.cushcity.com: An African-American online store featuring books, videos, music, toys, software, and more.

www.everythingblack.com: The place to find any- and everything black on the Net.

www.msbet.com: A Web site dedicated to more than music and entertainment: money, headlines, careers, lifestyles, health, and community. The official Web site for Black Entertainment Television.

www.netnoir.com: An afrocentric, afro-latin, afro-Caribbean, afro-European, African-American, and continental African Web site.

www.sistercircle.org: An up-and-coming Web site dedicated to all African-American women sister circles, reading clubs, organizations, and individuals for information and networking. Featuring event calendars with information on African-American authors, entertainers, empowerment conferences, and more.

www.sisterfriends.com: A Web site for African-American women.

ACKNOWLEDGMENTS

A special thank you for those who supported us in the development of *Going Off*.

Lara J. Asher, associate editor, for her expertise, and helping us grow this book from a bulb to a flower. Also thanks to Leia Vandersnick, assistant editor, for her commitment to helping to make this book become a reality.

Charles Palmer, Noreen's husband. Thanks so much for your love and spiritual inspiration. Your support is very much appreciated.

Kim Coleman and Debra Wade. Thanks for being there and helping Faye in the office.

To our sisters, our #1 cheerleaders. Linda Thomas and Gaynell Wicks, we love you.

To our big brothers, Al White, Carl White, John White. Thank you for serving as supporters and protectors over the years.

To the children: Rhiannon Childs, Kaci Childs, Michael Childs, Mathew Childs, Shawntell Smith, Charles Palmer, Jr., Arianna Palmer. We love you and thank you for giving us quiet time when we needed it.

Jamie Revelos-Beatty, Brenda Lovelace, Pam Free and Ron Cox, graphic support, word processing, and Web design. We are grateful for your enthusiastic support.

Wes Smith, Clara Villarosa, Monica Harris, Emma Rogers, Gina Benedict, Pam Delay, Vicki Eickelberger, George Fraser, the networking expert, and Jeremy Burdge, M.D. Thanks for your support and advice.

Jan Miller, agent. Thanks for your support.

Kent and Sarah Smith, photographers. Thanks for your attentiveness and expertise.

Special thanks to the extended family who have helped along the way: Brenetta Lovelace, Ora and James Hagood, Azilee Wade, and Evelyn White.

To our traveling partners: Toni Robinson, Yolanda Robinson, Barbara Thomas, Bing Rosecrans, and Carr Mel White—thanks for your support.

POSTSCRIPT

Contrary to the media, which sometimes portrays black female celebrities including First Lady Michelle Obama as angry black women, this book negates the stereotype that all black women are angry. Prior to the publishing of this book, there were several books on the market that portrayed the experience of white women and anger. Based on a gap in the literature, we decided to write the first book about women and anger from the perspective of black women. As human beings, we have the God-given gift of human emotion. Thus, one of the most unique aspects of being human includes the capability of experiencing a range of emotions. Therefore, this book is about the experience of black women and anger, an experience of human emotion. When channeled appropriately, it is at the high peaks of emotion when we reach our full potential or produce our best work. Consider the following situations where human beings worked from frustration toward motivation to achieve greatness: the Founding Fathers of our great country, *The Constitution of the*

United States of America, Rev. Dr. Martin Luther King Jr.'s famous *Letter from a Birmingham Jail* and *I Have a Dream Speech*, Dr. Maya Angelo, one of the first African American women to publicly discuss her personal life in her heralded book*, I Know Why the Caged Bird Sings*, and Nancy Brinker, a white woman who frustratingly started a foundation in loving memory of her sister, the Susan G. Komen Foundation.

Stereotypical notions of black women make it 'not ok' to talk intellectually about how black women can use their emotions and frustrations in a positive manner to create hope and change for our future. Feeding on the stereotype, people ask me the following question bearing a curious smile, "*You're the person that wrote that book about angry black women aren't you*?" Yes, I am the co-author, and, I silently say to myself in Sojourner Truth's speech style, *Ain't I a Woman*? Finally, in the spirit of Fannie Lou Hamer, Mary McLeod Bethune, Harriett Tubman, Coretta Scott King, Shirley Chisholm, Aretha Franklin, my sister Faye Childs, and many others, we all deserve respect as black women and I courageously stand with my sisters carrying a positive attitude that says "I can do all things through God who strengthens me."

-Noreen Palmer, MA, MSW, LISW

Listen to reading and lecture posted by ReadAloud – Ohio State University Libraries

library.osu.edu/blogs/readaloud/

www.youtube.com/watch?v=sBo-AyZva7U

Listen to the BlackBoard youtube video that promotes literacy: The Blackboard Presents: Buster Douglas Back In The Ring.- Knocking It Out

http://youtu.be/Fqjfa5MZHnA

Entertainment Staffer during book tour

To schedule a lecture and book signing email:

noreentherapy@gmail.com or visit

http://www.noreenpalmer.biz

Follow us on Twitter

Hit us on Facebook

Special

Thanks to

Our Family!

Noreen Palmer, MA, MSW

Noreen Palmer is a licensed psychotherapist practicing at Affirmative Counseling Associates in the greater Columbus, Ohio area. In addition she serves as Adjunct Instructor for Park University and has served as Guest Lecturer for The Ohio State University. Ms. Palmer has a solid background in social services, hospital administration and outreach. Utilizing her experience and passion for health education, Ms. Palmer founded first Annual Healthy Heart Luncheon with the National Coalition of 100 Black Women in Columbus Ohio. Palmer's achievements in health education and outreach include receiving the following recognitions: Recognition from US Department of Defense, Defense Logistics Agency for health presentation on Stress Management and annual listings in Who's Who publications including Who's Who in America, Who's Who Among American Women, Who's Who Among Healthcare Professionals, and Who's Who in the World. Ms. Palmer enjoys cooking, public speaking, and spending time with her family. For more information about Ms. Palmer's psychotherapy practice, visit: www.psychologytoday.com/noreenpalmer and www.noreenpalmer.biz.

Faye Childs

Faye Childs impacted the publishing industry in 1991 as the founder and creator of the BlackBoard African American Bestsellers List. The BlackBoard List created to give exposure to African American authors in the same way as the New York

Times Bestsellers List was a phenomenal success, books written by or about African Americans soared as publishers realized that this untapped market created an economic boon. After the BlackBoard List Childs went on to create The BlackBoard Awards held annually at Book Expo America, and the BlackBoard Book and Music Festival. Additionally Childs worked with the major houses such as Penguin Group USA, Random House, John Wiley and Sons, HarperCollins, Simon and Schuster promoting black authors to unprecedented success. The Book Industry Study Group, commissioned a study for ten years 1991 – 2001 to determine revenue generated by the BlackBoard List. The study determined that black book sales had become the fastest growth dynamic in all of publishing generating 2.5 billion dollars within that period of time. Today Childs is working towards the launch of a new social network called bittyblurb.com a web network connecting readers and books, building a fan base for all writers.